FUN Photo-Quilts & CRAFTS

For Barb!
Best wishes
Ami Simms

by Ami Simms

Thanks, Mom!

And very special thanks to...

Marsha McCloskey—soulmates as generous with their talent as Marsha are hard to find. If we lived in the same time zone we'd be dangerous.

The Hen Gang (alias Terry Blitchok, Linda Kay Bodker, Kathy Bradbury, Sue DeWitt, Patsy Hartz, and Phidge Sweers), Mary Andrews, Gina Angell, Sherry Bailey, Sharon Castle, Sophie Crittendon, Lucy Fazely, Nancy Jacoby, Terri Lamrock, and Mary Ellen Wojcik for allowing me to share their extraordinary talents with you.

Teresa Palmer, my "Executive Assistant" and friend, who created hours in the day for me to quilt and write by doing her job so well. I wouldn't have wanted to do it without you or the other elves in the office. Among your most endearing qualities? Your ability to find crucial bits of information I have momentarily misplaced in the garbage dump that is my desk, even though the only clue I can provide is: "I'm looking for something I wrote on a little piece of paper..."

Peggy Howard, the sister I never had, who sent frequent e-mails that almost always included an encouraging "How's the book coming?" Forgive me, Peg, for using all those symbols on top of the number keys in my replies.

Maggie DuPuis, from whom I've learned much about color and risk-taking, and who let me raid her stash whenever I felt needy. (If you think you're getting any of it back, forget it.)

Jim Booth and Richard Barclay, who can diagnose and cure my computer over the phone, severely limiting the number of excuses I can dream up for not working; David Small, for teaching me how to use my design software and providing much-needed technical support long after any sane person would have labeled me hopeless; the readers of my AfterChat Newsletter who sent their best snapshots when I ran out of faces to photo-transfer (their contributions are featured in "Let Me Have Your Best Shot" and "Shutterbugs"); the Guinea Pig Club, who took time out from their own quilting to proof the patterns and directions in this book; Linda Buzon, walking partner and confidant, who never once offered cheese with my whine; Christl Jelinek and Cindy Brick, who checked spelling, grammar, punctuation and did all they could so I wouldn't look quite so stupid; James B. Carlson and Lee Kirchner of C^3 Creative, for making the quilts on the cover look so good; Gary Lusk of Color Concepts, for translating my photographs to the printed page; and Lynn Rohkohl, Patrice Smith, John Loy and the rest of the fine people at Malloy Lithographing, for printing the book you're holding.

Finally, my love and thanks to my family—my husband, Steve, and our daughter, Jennie. Your sacrifices and good humor are the reason I lead a charmed life. I am truly grateful. I couldn't do any of this without you. And I wouldn't want to.

The author wishes to thank Corel Corporation for allowing her to use clipart from CorelDRAW!™.

The author assures the reader that the information in this book is accurate to the best of her knowledge, but assumes no liability or responsibility associated with its use, or the performance or quality of the goods or services cited herein.

Library of Congress Cataloging-In-Publication Data
Simms, Ami, 1954-
    Fun photo-quilts & crafts / by Ami Simms.
        p.   cm.
    ISBN 0-943079 -06-3 (trade pbk.)
        1. Patchwork.   2. Photographs on cloth.
        3. Textile printing.   4. Transfer-printing.
        I. Title.   II. Title: Fun photo-quilts and crafts.
    TT835.S532   1999   98-42763
    746.46--dc21   CIP

Published by MALLERY PRESS ● 4206 Sheraton Drive ● Flint, Michigan 48532-3557 USA

Contents

Preface 4
Introduction 5
Selecting Photographs 6
    What To Look For 6
    What About Copyright? 7
    Fixing Imperfect Pictures 8
    Organizational Hints 8
Sizing Photographs 8
    Sizing Templates 8
    Using Sizing Templates 9
Making Photo-Transfers 10
    To Transfer or Not to Transfer 10
    Enlarging & Reducing 10
    Calculating The Percentage 10
    Taping Photographs To Regular Paper 11
    Cropping Photographs 11
    Selecting Transfer Fabric 12
    At The Copy Machine 12
    Trimming & Pressing Transfers 12
    Trimming Finished Photo-Transfers 13
Understanding The Patterns 14
    Block Size/Quilt Size 14
    The Cutting Chart 14
    Assembly 15
Tips For Making Photo-Quilts 16
    Fabric 16
    Joining Patches 16
    Pressing 16
    Batting 17
    Basting 17
    Quilting 17
Basic Quilt Construction 19
    Preparation 19
    Cutting Fabric Strips 19
    Making A Sample Block 20
    Mitering Strips 20
    Joining Blocks & Sashing Strips 21
    Adding Borders 22
    Basting 22
    Binding 22
Gallery of Quilts 25
    "Mom's Wedding Day" 25
    "Heart & Flowers" 25
    "Cute As A Button" 26
    "Let Me Have Your Best Shot" 27
    "Photo-Transfer Teddy Bears" 28
    "Drewie & Bessie" 28
    "Star Within A Star Tote Bag" 28
    "Boys & Their Toys" 29

"Gone Fishin" 29
"Circle of Friends—The Hen Gang" 30
"The Eyes Have It" 30
"Sweet Dreams" 30
"Family Fotos" 31
"Shutterbugs" 32
"Mouse Pads" 33
"Coasters" 33
"Sophie's Vest" 33
"House Full of Memories" 34
"Lace Doily Ornaments" 35
"Wedding Pillow" 35
"Photo-Vests" 36
"The Men In My Life" 36
"In Pursuit" 37
"Photo-Transfer Neckties" 38
"Don't Fly Away" 38
"Jen's Photo Quilt Block" 39
"School Days" 39
"Kathleen's Kidlets" 40
The Patterns 41
    Watercolor 41
    Album 42
    Photo Album Cover 43
    Whirligig 44
    Snapshot 46
    Photo-Transfer Teddy Bears & Vests 49
    Photo-Transfer Neckties 49
    Variable Star 50
    Star Within A Star Tote Bag 52
    Trip Around The World 54
    Stacked Snowballs 55
    Snowballs & Nine Patches 56
    Square Within A Square 58
    Counterpane 60
    Counterpane Sheets & Pillowcase 62
    Mouse Pads & Coasters 63
    Embellished Vest 63
    Lace Doily Ornaments 63
    Pinwheel Star 64
    Hole In The Barn Door 66
    Log Cabin 68
    Shoo Fly 70
    Log Window 72
    Spinning Windmill 74
Resources 77
Spinning Windmill Pattern Template 79

Preface

I began quilting 25 years ago, unintentionally. I barely knew what a quilt was when I found myself sitting at an old-fashioned quilting frame in northern Indiana, with an Amish woman at each elbow. I had started the day by showing up at a barn raising unannounced, a letter in my hand from my faculty advisor assuring the Amish minister I hoped to meet that I was harmless. (I was. Really.)

We met, toured the barn, and soon discovered that a 20-year-old college girl from suburban Detroit and an Amish grandfather run out of things to talk about real fast. He suggested I go meet his wife who was attending a quilting bee at a neighbor's house. Since my goal for the day was to meet an Amish family, and somehow get them to ask me to come and live with them so I could write my thesis and graduate with a marketable skill—I was thrilled. (I had not yet figured out that a degree in anthropology is next to useless if one wants to eat.)

So, there I sat at the frame, staring at a quilt that looked more like a trampoline, with a dozen Amish women staring at me expectantly from beneath their starched white prayer caps.

They asked me if I wanted to quilt with them and I foolishly accepted the threaded needle they handed me. It wasn't long before they suspected I was clueless. They knew for sure when I declined their offer of a thimble and proceeded to ram the point of the needle into one finger and the eye of the needle into the other. I bled all over their quilt and they pulled out all my stitches after I left.

As it turned out, I did get to stay with the minister and his wife. She taught me to quilt, and it changed my life. I also learned how to milk cows and drive a horse and buggy. (Those activities didn't do a thing for me.) For some inexplicable reason I found quilting appealing, though painful. Over the years I persevered and have made over 100 quilts since those first tentative stitches.

My most recent interest has been working with photo-transfer quilts, first in preparation for writing *Creating Scrapbook Quilts*, and now with *Fun Photo-Quilts & Crafts*.

Work on this book began almost two years ago. As with most projects, I find the possibilities are so intriguing that it's hard to stop making the projects and start writing the book! There is always just one more thing to try. That was certainly the case for this book, which was supposed to be a lot shorter! There are still so many more possibilities to explore with photo-transfers I suspect I may just have to write *More Fun Photo-Quilts & Crafts,* or maybe *Son of Fun Photo-Quilts & Crafts*!

Sequel or not, if you find making photo-quilts as much fun as I do, let me hear from you. I'd love to see what you've made using this book as inspiration, or photo-quilt projects you've come up with on your own. Send pictures of what you've made to me at the address below.

If you give me permission when you send your snapshot, I'll scan your quilt and add it to the photo-quilts featured on my web site. Come take a look!

In the meantime, have fun and enjoy!

Ami Simms
c/o Mallery Press
4206 Sheraton Drive
Flint, MI 48532-3557
amisimms@aol.com
www.quilt.com/amisimms

Introduction

It's estimated that Americans took 18.2 billion photographs last year alone! Not all were as nice as the one above by Sherry Bailey, but even so, that's an awful lot of KODAK MOMENTS™. According to the Photo Marketing Association, the folks who keep track of stuff like that, 85.2% of all households claim to keep at least *some* of their photographs in albums.

Sure, some of *my* photographs are in albums, too. The rest are still in the flimsy paper envelopes from the photo lab, piled in a shoe box on the top shelf in the closet! I stick them in the albums once every two years when the pile tips over or I get such a bad head cold I don't mind inhaling the rubber cement fumes.

I used to feel guilty, but not any more. I've found a way to channel PAG (Photo Album Guilt) into creative self-expression. I make

photo-quilts! The process is easy and fun to do and the resulting quilts are infinitely more satisfying than paging through a photo album. Besides, if I really want to, I can do both. The transfer methods don't harm the original photographs, and, if I ever get around to it, I can still put the photos under protective plastic, complete with captions and dates. (Right, like I remember what year *that* picture was taken!)

Making a photo-quilt creates a copy of each cherished photograph in fabric. It's like having a spare—a thought I find comforting, since I've probably lost the negative anyway. Once the quilt is finished and hanging on the wall or draped over a bed, it can be appreciated much more often than any photo album.

Your quilt may even get a fair amount of attention from complete strangers. They're attracted to photo-quilts like magnets, oohing and aahing over pictures of people they've never met. Try sharing photos from your family reunion with people who weren't there. Unless they've got plans to show you an equally thick stack of snapshots of their new grandchild, you don't stand a chance. But, transfer those same pictures to fabric, sew them into a photo-quilt, and you will be surrounded by admirers.

Want the ultimate thrill? Give one away. Make a photo-quilt as a gift for someone you really care about and let 'em have it! Nothing comes close to the feeling you'll get when you give a gift that's appreciated so much. Weddings, anniversaries, graduations, or just because—here's your chance. A word of advice: include a handkerchief in the ribbon when you wrap the quilt. It'll come in handy for the tears when the package is opened.

Are you ready to have some fun? Let's get started! This book is organized in the same way you would go about making a photo-quilt. Be sure to read all the instructions before you start. (Just looking at the pretty pictures doesn't count!)

Selecting Photos

What To Look For

The best photo-quilts are made with the best photographs. Use only original photographs, not copies. Black and white photos can be used as well as color, and there's no law that says both kinds can't be used in the same quilt.

Root through your snapshots and pick the ones that are clear, sharp, in focus, and properly exposed. Look for photographs where the subject fills the frame and the background isn't cluttered.

A great photograph to transfer.

Avoid dark, under-exposed photos, no matter how cute they would have been if the flash had worked. *You may remember what's going on in the picture, but nobody else will have a clue.*

Skip this one.

Photographs with dog-eared corners, wrinkles and scuff marks will turn into transfers with these same imperfections. Individuals missing feet and heads will not grow replace-

ments when they are transferred to fabric. Subjects too tiny to identify in the picture won't be any easier to recognize in cloth.

Who is that kid?

Obviously, the better the original photograph the better the photo-transfer. However, if a crummy photo of some special person that absolutely *has* to be in the quilt is all you've got, then for goodness sake, take them out of the reject pile and don't worry. When all is said and done, that blurry, under-exposed snapshot of Uncle Harold that the dog got hold of will be just fine, as long as it's the only one with teeth marks and a missing corner. It might even be a conversation starter. Just make sure the rest of the photos are in better shape.

Want to obsess over picking the absolute "best" pictures, regardless of content? Take a close look at the photos in "Kathleen's Kidlets" on page 40. The photos with light backgrounds appear to make the quilt more 3-dimensional than those with darker backgrounds.

I point this out only because it's nice to know. As you can see, I chose pictures regardless of background color. I did have pictures with lighter backgrounds, but I figured Kathleen would much rather have pictures of her own kids in her quilt. I already have enough stress in my life.

What About Copyright?

Sometimes the best photographs in your stash are the best photographs in your stash because they were taken by a professional photographer! Be that as it may, they are protected by copyright laws. You're not supposed to make copies of them to use in your quilt without permission.

Wedding pictures taken by professional photographers, studio portraits, and school pictures are *verboten*, even though you've paid for them. Making copies can get you into hot water, not to mention embarrassing situations at the copy shop. While you may own the print, you don't own the right to make copies. In addition, photographs (and other images) in books, newspapers, and magazines are also copyright-protected. The owner of the copy machine will pull the plug if you attempt to copy anything that is copyright-protected.

Don't despair; there is a way out. Contact the photographer or studio and request permission. Most have standard "release forms" to give you. Be sure to detail exactly how you are going to use the photo, and let them know if it will be used for commercial purposes. That might make a difference. Take the release form with you to the copy shop.

For other photos, go to the source. Contact the editor of the newspaper or magazine or the publisher. Explain how the photo will be used, and get permission *in writing*.

It's faster to make an initial inquiry by phone, even though chances are you'll encounter an awful lot of people who don't know what a quilt is. Here's your chance to educate them. Large corporations hire people whose sole purpose in life is to say "no!" If that happens, don't take it personally, and be persistent. If you get a "no" just ask for the person's supervisor. Go as high up on the "food chain" as possible.

Nine times out of ten, you'll finally reach a friendly voice with the authority to say "yes!" When you do, get the correct spelling of their name, title, and complete address. Tell them to expect a short letter detailing what you want.

Ask them to sign the letter and return it to you. The easier you make it for them, the more likely they are to comply. The sooner they get the letter, the sooner they can grant permission. If you have a fax machine, use it.

Your Name
Your Address
Your City/State/Zip
Your Phone/Fax Number

Their Name & Title
Their Company Name
Their Address
Their City/State/Zip

Dear _____,

As I mentioned on the phone today, I would like to include the photograph of _____ which I found on page __ of your publication, entitled _____, in my photo-quilt. I will use the photograph to make a single quilt. It (will/will not) be used for commercial purposes.

If you will allow me to do this, please sign in the space provided below and return this letter to me in the enclosed envelope or by return fax.

Please contact me if you have any questions.

Sincerely,

_____
Their Name   Date

Your Name

An example of a letter that might be used to request permission to use copyrighted material from a publication.

Professional photographs taken before 1923 are more than likely all right to use, their copyright protection having expired; however, that is not always the case, so check first.

When you are unable to locate the owner of the copyright, you are taking a risk in having the image copied, as is the owner of the copy machine. They may not be willing to make copies for you without certain guarantees. Signing a waiver stating that you agree to take all responsibility should the owner of the copyright ever file a legal action, for example, may make them more inclined to take the risk.

Put it in writing. Begin with your name, address, and telephone/fax number. Write a letter describing the image in question and what you want to do with it—make a photocopy onto transfer paper and put the image on cloth. Address your letter to the copy shop and include this phrase:

> I assume any and all liability for the misuse, if any, in the making of a photocopy of the image described above, and release (name of establishment) from any liability and hold them harmless.

Remember: it's best to consult your attorney for legal advice, not a quilting book.

Fixing Imperfect Pictures

It's possible to improve some photographs, even after you've snapped the photo. You may not be able to erase the goofy look on someone's face, but you can make the photograph more suitable for transferring to cloth. If your camera turns people's eyes red, photo labs usually carry a special blue pen that can get most of the red out. A blue, water-soluble quilt marking pen will work in a pinch.

Some scuff marks on old black and white pictures can be erased with a soft gum eraser; just proceed cautiously. Creases on dark areas can be camouflaged somewhat with a soft lead pencil. Carefully mark the crease and smudge gently with a finger to make it less noticeable.

Organizational Hints

To make sure photographs borrowed from albums find their way back home again, write a description of the missing picture on a Post-it™ note and stick it right to the album page. If it hangs out over the edge you'll be able to tell at a glance that a picture needs to be replaced and which one goes where.

When borrowing photographs from others, label the back with the name of the owner. Do this with a Post-it™ note, too. Felt tip pens sometimes don't dry on the back of slick photo paper and can smear onto another picture very easily. Ball-point pens and too-sharp pencils can ruin a photograph by leaving ridges in it.

Sizing Photographs

Most of the projects in *Fun Photo-Quilts & Crafts* call for photo transfers that measure 3" square, finished size. This size keeps the blocks pleasing, yet manageable. It also reduces the cost of making the transfers. Six 3" x 3" photographs can easily fit on a single page of transfer paper. Since not every pattern calls for this same size, confirm the finished size of the transfer before beginning.

Sizing Templates

Subject matter and quality are the first considerations. Now it's time to worry about size. After you've assembled a pile of photos, look at them again, this time with a sizing template.

Make a sizing template out of sturdy plastic that you can see through. (It's not necessary to read a newspaper through it, just to see the general outline of the images in the photograph when the template is placed on top of it.) Take the finished photo-transfer size, in this case 3", and add ¼" on all sides. This will

make the actual template 3½" by 3½". Use a ruler and rotary cutter (with an old blade) to measure and cut the template all in one step, rather than marking a cutting line and using a pair of scissors. It will be much more accurate.

Then draw a square precisely ¼" in from the edge of the template. This will create a 3" square, centered inside the template, the same size as the finished transfer. (Similarly, if the finished transfer size is 3½", make the template 4" x 4" and draw a 3½" square inside.)

The outside dimension of the template is the cutting guide. Objects falling *inside* the square drawn on the template will be visible when the patchwork is sewn. Items falling *outside* the box will be hidden from view in the seam allowance. This template will be used to select and size photographs, to check the final size should photos be enlarged or reduced, and finally to cut the finished photo-transfers.

Mark the template with a fine point permanent marker. The "permanent" black line it makes on the side of the ruler can be removed easily with nail polish remover. (Just be careful not to get the acetone on the ruler lines or they will also be removed!)

Mark a small + in the center of the sizing template. That way, when you're busy admiring the adorable baby in the picture underneath, you'll be able to remember where the center of the image will be in the quilt patch. To help see the seam allowance, darken the ¼" seam allowance with the permanent black marker.

A sizing template.

Using Sizing Templates

To make certain the picture under consideration is right for the project, place the sizing template over it. Move it around until the subject is centered. Use the + as a guide.

The edge of the photograph *must* extend beyond the inner line of the sizing template. The amount it extends into the seam allowance is your margin for error. Never assume that the photograph is large enough if the image just meets the line. It must go beyond it.

Aim for at least a good ⅛" inch into the seam allowance. If the photograph does not extend far enough, there will be an ugly, bright white line visible after the ¼" seam is stitched and the patch is pressed into place.

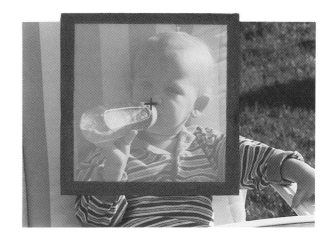

Using a sizing template.

Since cameras make rectangular photographs, and most photo-transfers need to be square, there will be extra picture left over. Hopefully, only boring backgrounds will be lost. With group shots, however, there is the danger of people on the far sides getting the ax.

Amateur photographers usually stand too far from their subjects, or cut off people's feet. Sometimes they do both! It might be difficult to find photographs with enough subject to fill the sizing template without including lots of sky overhead. There will probably be no shortage of people who stop at the knees.

Whatever the problem, enlarging or reducing the photograph will usually help. If you are sending the photograph out to be transferred professionally, make sure the company knows the finished size you desire.

Making Photo-Transfers

To Transfer Or Not To Transfer

There are several ways to transfer images to fabric. The most common and least expensive way is to copy photographs onto transfer paper using a color copy machine. (Yes, *color*. Even for black and white photos.) The photo-transfers featured in this book were all made with Photos-To-Fabric® transfer paper, except for a few of the photo-transfers in one quilt which were made with an inferior transfer paper. (Those stuck to the maker's iron!)

Original photographs were not harmed, and the resulting fabric images are washable, "iron-able" and right-reading. Both color and black and white photographs can be transferred to fabric successfully. If you prefer not to make the photo-transfers yourself, contact the firms listed on page 77 that will do this for you. Skip the rest of this chapter and we'll see you again on page 13.

Enlarging & Reducing

Not every picture will be the right size. Don't panic. Photographs can be enlarged or reduced to fit.

It's best to work from original photographs. Don't make enlargements or reductions on regular paper, then copy them to transfer paper. You'll be making a copy of a copy of a copy. The clarity of the photo-transfer is compromised with each generation removed from the original. Instead, enlarge or reduce the photographs directly on the photo-transfer paper after the exact size has been verified on "regular" paper first.

Calculating The Percentage

Most photocopy machines can reduce down to 25% or enlarge up to 400%. Stay below 200%, or twice the size of the original. Not only are imperfections magnified, but photos can look grainy if enlarged too much. Don't

forget, the pictures will be printed on fabric, not glossy photo paper. The weave of the cloth will be visible.

Enlarging and reducing is as easy as pushing a button. Getting the picture to come out the right size is the tricky part. There are three ways enlargements and reductions of the correct size can be made:

First is the trial and error method. The operator of the copy machine guesses at the size and pushes a button. You check what the machine spits out with your sizing template and try again if it's the wrong size.

The second option is to do the math yourself using the simple formula below:

$$\frac{\text{The size you have}}{\text{The size you want}} \times \frac{100\%}{X\%}$$

The third option, for those of us who would rather stick our head in an oven than perform mathematical calculations of any kind, is to use a proportional scale or wheel. These are available at large office supply stores, quick printers, and blueprint supply stores.

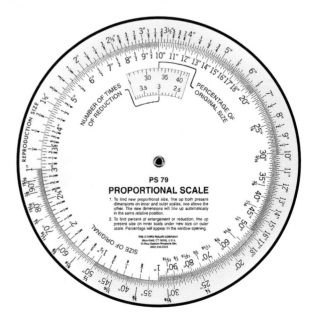

A proportional scale.

10

For most of the projects in this book, the desired measurement of the finished photo-transfer is 3¼" x 3¼". (Don't forget that the image must go *beyond* the seam line.) Find the 3¼" mark on the larger outside wheel that says "Reproduction Size."

Measure the width or height of the original picture, whichever is shorter. Locate that measurement on the smaller inside wheel labeled "Size of Original." Turn one or the other wheel until these two measurements line up exactly and the percentage of enlargement or reduction will appear in the little window.

The person operating the copy machine can punch the percentage into the machine and create the exact size you need. (Take the sizing template with you, just in case. It would be a shame to be mathematically correct and take home a transfer just a hair off due to a mechanical quirk.)

Photocopy machines print all the images on a page the same way. They can't pick and choose, enlarging one, reducing another, and keeping the rest an exact copy. So, all the photographs that need to be photocopied at 130% of the original size, for example, need to be presented to the copy machine at the same time. All those copied at 100% (the size of the original) need to be grouped together as well.

Therefore, take time to organize photographs by size before heading to the copy machine. One marathon copy session will be more economical than having to make several trips, especially when several enlargements or reductions could have been done at the same time.

Taping Photographs To Regular Paper

The first order of business is to transport your photographs to the color copy machine. Carrying them loose in an old shoe box means you and the operator of the copy machine will have to take the time to arrange them when you get there. Even if you're the only one in the store and Mother Theresa is working the machine, you'll wish you had arranged the photographs at home first.

Tape them to plain white paper measuring 8½" by 11", the same size as the transfer paper. Put one or two pieces of Scotch™ removable double-coated tape under each photo to hold the pictures in place until you need to take them off the paper and put them back in the album. The tape comes off very easily and can even be placed on the glossy sides of snapshots, for a short time. (Don't leave it on longer than a day or so, and store it in a cool place.)

Place the tape under the darkest parts of the photograph to prevent phantom marks from appearing on the transfer paper. (Sometimes the light of the copy machine is so bright it penetrates the photograph and "reads" the tape underneath as part of the image to copy.)

The ideal is to position six photographs per sheet of paper. Butt the images edge to edge, as no seam allowances are required at this step. Do leave ¼" around the entire outside edge of the paper, however. Most color copiers cannot print all the way to the edge of the paper. Any images you put there will not come out.

Group black and white photographs together on the same page. Group color photographs together also. If you can, group photographs with similar exposures (all light/all dark) too. Color copy machines take exposure readings at various places on the page and then average them together. If you have five dark pictures and one light one all on the same page, for example, it will be more difficult for the machine to take an accurate reading.

Group those pictures that need to be reduced to the same percentage on the same page. Group those that need to be enlarged as well, but keep in mind that you can't fill an entire page with enlargements. While they may fit on the page used to transport them to the copy machine, once they are enlarged they may not fit on the transfer paper! Plan accordingly.

Cropping Photographs

Not all your pictures will fit on the paper. That's almost a given. The easiest thing to do is to cut off the parts of the photos that you don't need to make the photo-transfer. Use the sizing template as a guide, trim off extra sky or extraneous backgrounds, or people over on the sides of pictures that you just don't like any more.

If the pictures don't belong to you, or you have some moral objection to cutting photographs, simply let the part of the picture you don't need hang off the edge of the paper. It won't copy and you won't have to cut it.

It's also legal to layer pictures one on top of the other to fit the most number of pictures possible on a single page. Don't forget that pictures can be placed upside-down or sideways to get the most per page. Just tape them in place securely, and remember to remove any tape from the glossy side of the pictures as soon as possible after the transfers are made.

Position as many pictures per page as possible.

Selecting Transfer Fabric

White smooth fabric works the best. The higher the thread count the better. Two hundred thread count cotton is optimum. Use it right off the bolt, without washing it first. Washing will just soften the fabric and make the little cotton fibers pop up. Even that minute amount of fuzz can have an adverse effect on the transfer. Don't worry, once the transfer is on the fabric shrinkage will not be a problem.

The transfer paper essentially releases a transparent film with color in it. It must be "printed" on white fabric for the true colors of the original photograph to come through. Similarly, if the fabric is not white, the color of the fabric will impact the photo-transfer. For example, while it is possible to transfer to muslin, everyone in the picture will look slightly tanned. Worse yet, muslin with the little brown flecks will make your grandmother look like she has acne. Transfer onto green fabric and everyone will look seasick. You get the idea.

At The Copy Machine

Take the Photos-To-Fabric® transfer paper and your photographs (taped to regular paper) to a place that has a color copy machine. Large office supply stores, quick printers, even some libraries, shipping services and grocery stores have them. This transfer paper will only work in color copy machines, not black and white copiers, not computer printers, and not the new combination fax/printer/copy machines. It must be a color copy machine.

Color copy machines are wonderful. A knowledgeable technician can not only use one to make an exact color reproduction, but can punch a few buttons and actually improve on the original. Brightness, contrast and color can all be manipulated if needed. Just ask.

Check each copy against the original to make sure the color is just right. Since size is also critical, measure each copy with the sizing template before heading home.

Trimming & Pressing Transfers

After the original photographs have been copied to the transfer paper, cut each image apart. Cut off any part of the transfer that is not needed, especially white borders around photographs and the outside white edge that the color copier didn't print on.

Press the white cotton fabric that will receive the transfer. It is important to remove any moisture and to remove *all* the wrinkles. The center crease probably won't come out easily, so work around it.

If a transfer is ironed over a crease, the crease will be as permanent as the people in the picture. Unfortunately, creases usually manifest themselves in the most obvious places, making family members in your quilt look as though they've got dents in their foreheads or the ability to bend at the chest, so make sure all the wrinkles are out before you start. (Should a transfer crease *after* it has been ironed to fabric, just press it with a warm iron.)

The best surface on which to iron transfers is a piece of flat wood with a layer or two of quilt batting on top. Wrap an old pillow case or a piece of muslin around it and put it on the floor. Putting the ironing surface as low as possible will give you the best leverage.

Check the padding periodically. Cotton batting will compress over time, polyester batting will melt, and before you know it your slightly padded ironing surface is hard as a rock. Replace the batting and press on.

No spare chunks of wood hanging around? A cloth mouse pad is a good, inexpensive, short-term substitute for small transfers. After many transfers, however, it will lose its bounce and develop dents and divots from the pressure of the iron. Just replace it with another.

Place mouse pads on a hard floor over newspapers or an old piece of fabric. (Sometimes the rubber bottom of the mouse pad will stain the floor.) Try not to inhale the mouse pad fumes while ironing; that can't be a good thing. And don't ignite the newspaper!

What about a heat press? Unless it comes with an air compressor, you'll get better transfers with your iron. The 100 pounds of pressure put out by most home heat presses is distributed over the *entire* bed of the press, not per inch. Using a regular iron, you'll be concentrating your energies on the surface area of the iron, a much smaller area. In addition, home heat presses may not have the right padding. Too fluffy or too flat can make a difference.

Press each image for 30 seconds, or according to package instructions, on the hottest setting the fabric will allow. No steam. Move the iron often to keep the steam vents from resting in the same place during the entire transferring time. Take the iron away, and peel off the backing paper.

The more pressure behind the iron, the better the transfer. Don't fret. While it is necessary to press hard, weight lifting doesn't need to be your next hobby. My 15-year-old daughter, who can get the scale to read 100 pounds if she jumps on it, does just fine.

Trimming Finished Photo-Transfers

Now that the transfers have been made, it's time to trim them to size. Check the pattern again to see what size the photo-transfer patch should be, and cut it accordingly.

To help center the image, tape the sizing template to the back of your rotary ruler, lining up one side with the edge of the ruler.

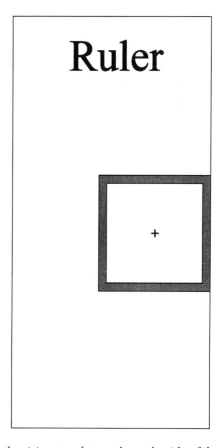

Tape the sizing template to the underside of the ruler.

13

Trim photo-transfers with sizing template.

With the template taped firmly to the ruler, place it over the image. Center the + sign over the center of the image, then check to make sure that the image extends well into the seam allowance. Trim the first side. Then turn the image 180°. Line up the freshly trimmed side with the opposite side of the sizing template. Check to make sure that the image extends into the seam allowance and make the second cut parallel to the first.

Turn the photo-transfer again to cut the third side. Make sure the freshly cut edges are parallel to the lines of the rotary ruler and the image is within the seam allowance. Your third cut will make a perfect right angle.

Turn the photo-transfer a fourth and final time to make the last cut, again making sure that the trimmed seams are parallel and that the image goes into the seam allowance.

Cut the rest of the photo-transfers for the quilt in this manner. Treat them as just another patch when following the construction guides in the pattern section.

Understanding The Patterns

Block Size/Quilt Size

Each quilt pattern gives the size of the finished block. Check your completed blocks against this measurement to make sure they are sewn accurately. Use this measurement to calculate the size of quilts with more (or less) blocks, or a different configuration.

Also included is the finished size of the quilt, rounded *up* to the nearest inch. The amount of quilting, type and thickness of batting, fabric, and shrinkage that may occur with laundering, are all factors that can change the size of the finished quilt. Your quilt should be within ½" either way of the size listed. (You'll know your quilt is the "right" size when everything lays reasonably flat, your points come pretty darn close, and you are filled with an enormous feeling of satisfaction.)

Each pattern also notes the size of the finished photo-transfer. This measurement will be needed to make the sizing template described on pages 8 and 9. The amount of transfer paper required for each project is listed, too. The assumption here is that enlargements or reductions are not necessary and that the original photographs are already the right shape or can be cut or layered to fit six pictures per page of transfer paper. If this is not the case, adjust accordingly.

The Cutting Chart

Start on the left, identifying the part of the quilt to cut. Move to the right to find the following information:

Quantity. The number in the chart here refers to the total number of that piece needed to make the entire quilt as pictured. Sometimes there will be two numbers separated by a comma. That's because there are probably two patches the same size to cut. (Look left.) The double numbers will usually carry through the chart all the way to the yardage. The first number listed in one column always corresponds to the first number listed in all subsequent columns. (See the Log Cabin pattern on page 68, for example.)

When there are two numbers separated by a comma in the Quantity column and they are *not* the same size, (border pieces, for example) the strip width is the same, but the length is different. To see how long to cut the piece, look under Dimension where you will most likely find two measurements, one for each pair of border pieces. (Go back to the Log Cabin pattern and take another look.)

A "2" in the lining column indicates a pieced lining. Stitch the two lining pieces together, running the seam horizontally across the back of the quilt. (Snapshot and Hole In The Barn Door require a single piece of lining fabric, however if that fabric is *less* than 44" wide it may need to be pieced also.)

Dimension. This is the exact shape that needs to be cut. Don't come close; cut exactly. Invest in the best ruler possible. Skimp here and you'll pay later on.

Sometimes the shape in the diagram is obviously a triangle and the dimension the chart says to cut is a square. Don't worry. The directions that follow the cutting chart will show you how to get the shape needed.

Strip Width. Quick rotary cutting methods are used throughout the book. The first step is to cut a strip in the width indicated. See page 19 to learn how to cut accurate strips.

No. of Strips and **Yield/Strip.** These numbers will tell how many strips to cut as well as the number of patches each strip will yield. The calculations are based on fabric 44/45" wide with a wide selvage edge, a high degree of shrinkage, and a hefty margin for error. It is assumed the fabric will be folded in quarters and cut four layers at a time. The largest patch cut from the folded fabric was calculated at a minuscule 10". The yield per strip can surely be increased on some patches if the fabric is unfolded. However, this takes longer and the savings are minimal. Life is short!

Strips which need to be pieced together to create long sashing strips and/or borders have no Yield/Strip. See page 20 for a slick way to join strips.

These two sections, and the yardage section below, presume that each patch listed will be cut from the same chunk of fabric. Since most quilts look best with *many* different fabrics, not just two, the information is presented only as a reference point, a place from which to start. The number of strips to cut and their yield will obviously vary according to the number of different fabrics in the quilt.

Yards. This is the approximate yardage needed to make the quilt pictured. Keep in mind that I cut fabric in its folded state, four thicknesses at a time. Also, I'm *very generous* with yardage. I include shrinkage, an inch or so to re-align after multiple cuts in case your ruler drifted, and a wee bit of room to "fudge."

Besides, I've never been too keen on buying small amounts of fabric. (You should see my stash!) The smallest chunk of fabric I buy is usually ⅓ yard. (I won't tell you my largest!) I've never been sorry I bought a little extra fabric. I love leftovers—as long as they are not the kind that live in the refrigerator!

Assembly

Step-by-step instructions follow the Cutting Chart. Remember that patches should be sewn in alphabetical or numerical sequence according to the diagrams. Unless otherwise noted, all seam allowances are ¼". All patches should be placed right sides together, with raw edges even, for every seam.

Once the instructions for a particular block are given, the rest of the quilt construction is fairly basic and straightforward. It is also virtually identical for every quilt. Rather than waste time and space in each pattern with redundant information, I've included a section called Basic Quilt Construction. It contains information on how to cut strips, join blocks and sashing strips, add borders, and bind a quilt. It certainly is no substitute for a good basic book on quiltmaking, but should help the beginner.

Tips For Making Photo-Quilts

Fabric

When picking fabric for a photo-quilt, just about anything goes. Photo-transfers have a unique chameleon-like quality and will "go" with just about any color fabric. Think about contrast instead. Follow the indications for "light," "medium," and "dark" fabrics in the patterns and study the quilts on pages 25-40.

The only quilt that gave me "color trouble" was "Shutterbugs." (See page 32). The strong black and white prints (no "color") overpowered the photo-transfers. They got lost in the shuffle. So, I replaced them with photo-transfers of people wearing very bright, vibrant colors, especially red.

I realize most people would probably opt for keeping their current set of friends or relatives and changing their fabric, but I had my heart set on using the collection of black and white fabrics I'd been saving for years, and I had a few extra pictures from my newsletter readers. Moral of the story? Any color scheme will work *except* black and white. If you insist on using black and white, make sure the people in the pictures are flashy dressers!

Joining Patches

When stitching a photo-transfer to "regular" fabric, place the photo-transfer on the top whenever possible. This will compensate for the fact that the photo-transfer will not stretch one iota and the patch it is sewn to will probably stretch a little or a lot. Most sewing machines tend to feed the fabric on the bottom (closest to the feed dogs) at a slightly faster rate of speed than the fabric on the top. Putting the "stretchier" fabric on the bottom will ease it in.

Sometimes that's not possible, in which case it's a good idea to pin the two pieces of cloth together. Just remember never to stick pins in the part of the photo-transfer that will be seen. Pin only in the seam allowances.

A word about un-joining patches: Don't. Let me amend that: try not to rip out seams, unless it's absolutely necessary. Fixing a mistake before it compounds itself is a good thing, but sewing the seams in the first place leaves little holes in the photo-transfer which are visible to the naked eye. Ripping the seam obviously removes the thread. No thread, and you'll see the holes even without your glasses!

What to do? Either re-stitch the seam by planting the needle in the same exact holes made by the needle originally (stop laughing!) or move the tip of a hot iron over the holes in the photo-transfer to partially close them.

Photo-transfers, by nature, are a little stiffer than regular fabric. The threads of the cloth are fused in place under the transfer and unable to wiggle to one side of the needle or the other as it penetrates the fabric. Often the needle pierces the thread instead of gliding around it. Many sets of needle holes will eventually weaken the fabric to the point where it isn't strong enough to be used in the quilt. Therefore, two ripped seams on the same photo-transfer patch is the limit. Three attempted seams and it's out. Make another photo-transfer and start over.

Pressing

Convention dictates that seams should be pressed under the darkest patch. They're less likely to be noticed there. That's a good rule. For photo-quilts there's another rule that is even more important: always press *away* from the photo-transfer patch. Since that patch is slightly stiffer, it makes sense not to have to fold it back on itself. Press away from it, and seams will lay flat and stay that way. Most of the time they will be hiding under the darker patch anyway. When these two rules conflict, press *away* from the photo-transfer patch.

Just as importantly, make sure the pressing strategy is followed consistently throughout the entire block, and from block to block as well. Keeping the pressing strategy consistent will make the whole block go together more easily. It will actually be possible to slide and lock patches in place before sewing, assuring that corners match for perfect intersections.

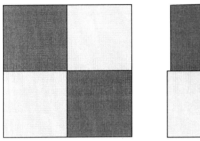 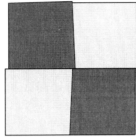

Good.............................. and not-so-good.

Here's how that "slide and lock" process works. The dark patch with the seam allowance under it is physically higher. The seam allowance actually pushes it up. The patch without is lower. When four patches are joined, the light/dark patches alternate. If the pressing has been consistent, it is possible to slide the two together until the higher patch stops the low one from passing beyond the point where they line up perfectly. Look at the seam from the wrong side. You'll see something like this when seams match properly:

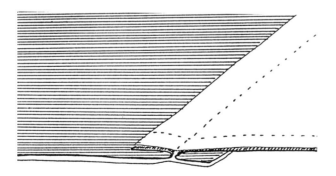

Seam allowances locked into perfect position.

Batting

Thin batting is best for photo-quilts. It will still show off miles of quilting, and the quilt will lay flat on bed or wall. Fluffy batting will create steeper hills and deeper valleys as the quilting thread passes through it. Shadows may appear in unwanted places, and people in the pictures may take on an expression of having just finished a large meal.

Basting

Baste before quilting, just don't baste through the photo-transfers. It's more than a little spooky sticking a pin right through somebody's head, and while body piercing is ever so popular right now, I don't even like driving sharp objects through *pictures* of limbs and torsos. Besides, basting through the photo-transfers will leave a hole. While the hole can be reduced significantly with a hot iron, it will never close completely. It's best not to create one in the first place.

Quilting

Photo-transfers don't mind being quilted at all. Skip them and you'll miss one of the most exciting parts of making a photo-quilt.

I prefer to quilt them by machine, after I've gone ¼" around all the seam lines with my walking foot. Then I "free-motion quilt" by dropping the feed dogs and guiding the quilt under the needle myself, instead of letting the machine do all the work.

Use clear nylon thread top and bottom. It will save you hours of fussing with the thread tension. Wind the bobbin only half full to keep your machine from making funny noises as it winds. (Regular thread can be used in the rest of the quilt, in contrasting or matching color. Or continue with the nylon thread, as you like.)

Call your sewing machine dealer to find the needle appropriate for your machine for the thread you intend to use. Usually a needle with an elongated eye is helpful to keep the thread from building up heat as it passes through. Larger round-eyed needles will accomplish the same thing, but will leave a bigger hole.

It's absolutely essential to see as much of the quilt as possible while free-motion quilting. Remember that the quilt will be moving in all directions, including backwards. A spring-loaded darning foot with a really wide open area in the center, or an "open toe," is ideal. My Bernina likes her #29 foot. Or, try a Big Foot®. Adapter shanks make it possible to use this versatile foot on almost every sewing machine. (See Resources.)

Quilt around the areas of highest contrast. It's easier to see, so there's less of a chance for error. Outline quilt around clothing and bodies, and anything in the background that has a line to follow—doorways, furniture, curtains, picture frames, etc. Use a pencil to highlight areas that need to be quilted but are hard to see. (On dark areas look for the reflection of the graphite, not the color of the line.)

Fluffy trees and curly hair can be "outlined" too; just switch from straight lines and long curves to choppy, zigzagged needle placements. Stay away from faces. Quilting around eyes, noses, and lips just makes a person look goofy.

The picture below was photographed with light shining behind the quilt. Study the quilting possibilities.

Quilting detail from "Snapshot."

Keep people in the photo-transfers facing up. They're actually easier to quilt around when they're right-side-up and not standing on their heads. That's because it's easier to anticipate the path of the needle. If people stood on their heads more often in real life, this wouldn't be a problem, but until they do, don't turn the quilt upside-down.

Your imagination should be your guide when quilting photo-transfers. There are really no hard and fast rules, as each and every photo transferred to fabric is unique. Quilt a little or a lot; it's up to you. You'll be creating a new quilting strategy with every picture. That's what keeps it exciting!

As you quilt from one part of an image to another, stop occasionally to rest and plan ahead. Always stop with the needle in the down position, otherwise the next stitch in the series could be a very long one if the quilt is accidentally moved between stops and starts.

Concentrate on even stitches, although the path the thread takes is more important than the size of the stitch. Vary the speed of the machine and the speed at which the quilt is guided under the needle until you find the right combination. Slower speeds and smaller stitches are acceptable, as long as the stitches are not so small that the photo-transfer is perforated. Success comes with practice.

Support the quilt on an extra table as you work. There's nothing worse than having the weight of a falling quilt unexpectedly alter the quilting path from one that goes *around* your niece's head to one that goes *through* it. Ouch!

Remember that photographs and photo-transfer patches are 2-dimensional. They're flat and we're used to seeing them that way. Once they're quilted, they become 3-dimensional. The natural hills and valleys made by the stitches change the appearance of all the fabrics in a quilt, including the fabric with pictures on it. Waves in a calico print are hardly noticeable. Waves in your grandmother's face are more so. Because the photo-transfers are stitched into a quilt, this means they will never ever lie completely flat. This slight distortion is part of the process. It can't be helped. Don't let it drive you crazy.

Basic Quilt Construction

What follows are my favorite construction strategies—the ones I use when I make my own quilts. They are procedures I've incorporated into my quiltmaking, gleaned from over 20 years of experience learning from other quilters and from my own mistakes. They are presented here as an aid for the beginning quilter who has had little or no experience building a quilt. They don't cover every facet of quiltmaking and are not meant to be a substitute for a quilting mentor, a beginning class, or one of the many fine quilting books written specifically for beginning quilters.

Preparation

Clean the sewing machine, oil it according to the manufacturer's instructions, and put in a new needle. Measure the distance from the needle to the side of the presser foot that will guide the ¼" seam. *Is it really a quarter of an inch?* Use a ruler to check and make sure. Then sew something to see if the stitched seam measures exactly ¼". If not, adjust the sewing machine, the driver, or both.

Use thread that either matches one of the fabrics being stitched, or a neutral color thread. Bright white isn't a neutral color; neither is black. Beige or tan is a better alternative. When sewing sashing strips or border pieces together, use an exact match, even in the bobbin. It may take a few extra moments to re-thread the machine, but it's a little detail that can make a big difference.

Cutting Fabric Strips

Just about every pattern in this book requires cutting strips. These strips will either be cut again to make patches, or stitched one to the other to create sashing strips or borders. In either case, learning to cut them quickly and accurately will save time and money. The trick is in the preparation and in the folding.

Whenever strips are required, cut them from 44/45" wide fabric that has been washed, dried and ironed. (When ironing, move the iron parallel to the selvage edge, not perpendicular to it. The fabric will then be far less likely to stretch out of shape.)

Folding the fabric accurately will ensure that strips will be consistently straight from end to end. Strips with kinks or four distinct segments cannot be used for sashing and borders, but may be suitable for patches.

First fold the fabric in half by bringing both selvage edges together. Hold the fabric at the fold, grasping it with the index finger and thumb of each hand. Gently roll the fabric back and forth at this fold until the selvage edges are parallel. Don't worry if the edges on the sides are way off. That just means the fabric may not have been wrapped and/or cut straight off the bolt. That is precisely why rolling the fold is better than just grabbing two corners and holding them together to make the first fold.

Then, when the selvage edges are parallel, lay the fabric on a flat surface. The cloth should be completely flat, without puckers or ripples at the fold.

Now bring the selvage edges up to the fold. Position them at the fold, adjusting left or right as needed so that there are no ripples or waves at the "new" fold.

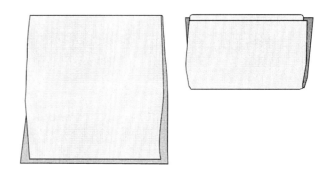

Fold fabric in half, then in half again.

Place the fold against one of the horizontal lines of the cutting mat. I can usually see the fold closest to me the best. Trim the ragged edges off.

I like to use both hands when cutting strips. The first cut, to even off the raw edge, is made with my "stupid" (non-dominant) hand. All subsequent cuts are made with my "smart" (dominant) hand. I don't have to flip the fabric around and re-align it, or walk to the other side of the cutting table. Get a rotary cutter that can be used with either hand, without unscrewing the blade, and you can do this too.

Here's the drill for right-handed quilters. (Lefties, do the opposite.) Place the ruler on the left side of the fabric. Line it up with a line on the cutting mat. Make sure all four layers are peeking out beyond the edge of the ruler and whack them off with your left hand.

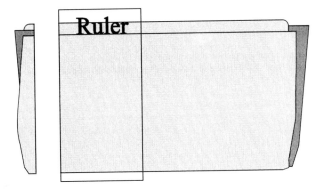

Trim the fabric with your "stupid" hand.

Now, slide the ruler over to the left so that it covers a strip of the desired width. Cut the strip with your right hand.

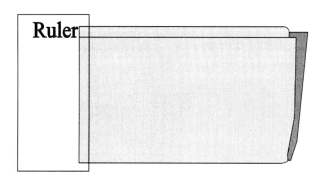

Cut the strips with your "smart" hand.

Unfold the strip to make sure that it is straight and without kinks. If so, continue cutting strips. If not, re-fold and try again.

20

Making A Sample Block

Always make one complete block before proceeding with the remaining blocks in the quilt. It's your safety net. Use it to check your color combinations, to confirm seam allowance and block size, and to make sure that the patches are cut accurately. If everything works out perfectly, terrific—one less block to make. If not, take the time to figure out what went wrong and fix it before going on. One "wasted" block now can save lots of heartache later.

Mitering Strips

Marsha McCloskey showed me this painless way to miter strips of any width together. Lay the two strips to be joined right sides up on the cutting mat so they overlap 1" more than their width. Huh?! OK, let's say you have two 1½" strips. Lay them down so they overlap by 2½". (It doesn't matter which one is on top.)

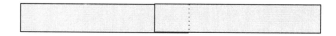

Lay the strips on the cutting mat so they overlap.

Place the ruler at an angle approximating 45° (*any* angle will work) on the overlap. The ruler doesn't have to line up with anything. As long as the ruler's edge will guide a cut that will slice through both pieces of fabric completely, the miter will work. Now cut.

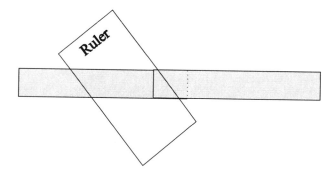

Cut at about a 45° angle.

Discard the corners that fall off. Place the two cut edges right sides together, and sew ¼" from the raw edge. The little triangles that pop up at the top and bottom of the seam should guide your stitching.

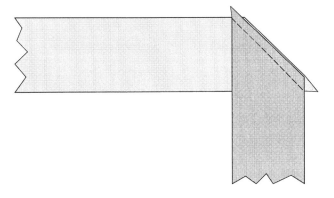

Sew the two strips together with a ¼" seam.

Since both pieces are cut at the same time, any angle will always create a perfect match without measuring or marking!

After the strips have been spliced together this way, press the seam allowances to one side and iron out the folds. The strips have been cut cross-grain, so they will stretch if handled too much. Measure and cut them on a flat surface.

Joining Blocks and Sashing Strips

Lay all the blocks, sashing strips and set squares (if any) on the floor and get a good look at them. Assign a letter to each column.

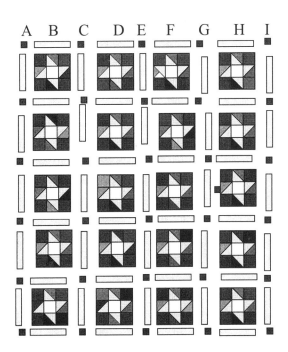

Arrange blocks and assign each column a letter.

Once the most pleasing configuration has been decided upon, gather the pieces up. Stack them in order, column by column, keeping the ones in the top row on the top of each stack.

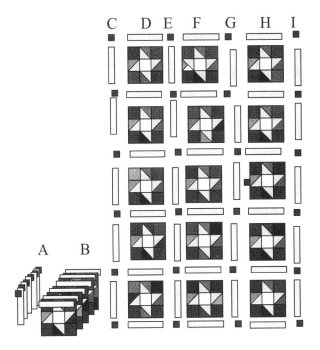

Gather up the pieces in order.

Bring the first two stacks over to the sewing machine. Keep them in the same orientation. Don't accidentally turn them a quarter turn or things may not look as you had planned. (It may help to label the stacks if the sewing process will take more than a few hours and the stacks have to be stored and then retrieved again for the next sewing session.)

Sit down at the sewing machine. Put stack **A** on your left thigh and stack **B** on your right thigh. Take the sashing strips, set squares, or blocks off the piles in order, one at a time from each thigh. Place them right sides together. Chain sew them together. Feed them under the presser foot one pair after the other, with about a ¼" space in between. Do not cut the threads; instead leave them joined.

Now, place the joined units on your left thigh, and stack **C** on your right thigh. After stack **C** is added, put the joined units on your left thigh and put stack **D** on your right thigh. Work through the stacks in this way until all are joined. (Breathe a *thigh* of relief.) Do not clip any of the threads.

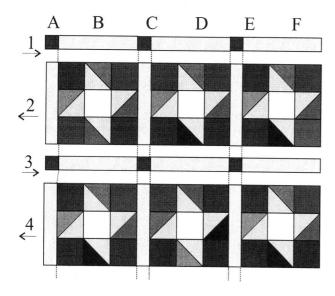

Chain sew the units together column by column.

After all the stacks are joined, press the seam allowances. Press all seam allowances in row 1 to the right. Press them to the left in row 2. Keep alternating the seam allowances left and right so when the rows are joined the seam allowances will "lock" and points will match.

After the seam allowances are pressed, sew long seams to join the rows. Keep track of which way the seam allowances are supposed to go for perfect joins. (The stitching between blocks can be clipped as you sew the long seams if you find it easier to manipulate the seam allowances this way.) Press all the long seams in one direction.

Adding Borders

Add the borders along the top and bottom of the quilt first, then add the ones on the sides. It's often possible to add a single strip across these shorter sides of a quilt top without piecing, if it's done first. If the borders are added along the *sides* first and *then* the top and bottom are added, I find I'm not always that lucky. All the measurements in the cutting chart assume that you agree with me.

It's a good idea to measure the quilt top, then check the cutting chart to see how close it is to reality before cutting any border pieces. If you're off by a little, it can be eased in. If you're off by a lot, adjust the measurement, then cut the strips. On long seams (longer than a foot) it's a good idea to pin every 6" or so. After stitching each border, press the seam allowances towards the border.

Basting

Whether you baste on an old fashioned frame of 1 x 2s and C-clamps like I do, or baste on the floor, or drape your quilt sandwich over a Ping-Pong table and pin it every 5 or 6 inches with little brass safety pins, do something to keep the three layers together during the quilting process. Nothing else will ensure that the quilt remains pucker-free and without distortion. The more you baste, the better.

Binding

Cut binding strips 2½" wide using cross-grain strips, folding and cutting like it says to do on pages 19 and 20. Join the strips using Marsha's slick mitering method (page 20) and press seam allowances to one side. Bring the two long edges together, fold, and press. This eliminates any fussing with raw edges when the binding is turned over the edge of the quilt and stitched down. That's the plan.

The number of strips needed to bind the quilts in this book has been calculated for you. I was forced to actually figure out a system to do that! (No, the numbers didn't just come to me in a dream.) Even though I am a non-mathematical person, this works:

First, add the lengths of the four sides of the quilt to bind. Add 10". (That's 4" to turn the corners—1" for each corner—and 6" to overlap or join the beginning to the end.) The number you come up with is the total number of inches required to bind the quilt. Write it down some place.

Next, assume that the usable width of 44/45" fabric is really only 42" after laundering. From that 42", the overlap (width plus 1") must be deducted: *once* from the first and the last strip, and *twice* from the middle strip(s).

Imagine that the binding is made up of a first strip (A), a last strip (Z), and an unknown number of middle strips (X).
When added together, they are equal to or greater than the sides of the quilt, plus the additional 10".

Here's how to figure it out. **A** is the usable width of the fabric minus the width of the strip plus the 1" overlap, or in this case 42" - 3½". So, **A** = 38½". **Z** is the same as **A**.

X is the usable width of the fabric minus width of the fabric plus the overlap twice. (Remember **X** is joined to other strips on *both* ends.) That's 42" - 7". So **X** = 35".

Turn on the calculator. Add 38.5 plus 38.5 (taking care of **A** and **Z**). Now add 35 as many times as it takes to reach or exceed the number of inches you need to bind the quilt. My desk calculator has a button that turns the printer on and off. One click past "print" is something that says "IC." If you turn that feature on, it will print out the number of things it added together. That is very handy because that's also the number of strips you need to cut. Voila!

Now that you know the formula, you can use it to calculate any width binding on any quilt. It will also get you pretty close to the right number of strips to cut for border pieces too. At this point you are either empowered or confused. In either case, let's move along and see how to attach the binding to the quilt.

After you sew the strips for the binding together, don't measure the entire length, reference the cutting chart in the pattern, and cut the binding to size. Stitch it to the quilt first, then cut off what you don't need.

Put the walking foot or even feed attachment on your machine. Cut one end of the binding at a 45° angle and bring it to the middle of one of the sides. Leaving a 3" "tail" of binding, begin stitching it to the quilt using a ⅜" seam allowance. This is just slightly wider than "normal," but it looks more balanced to my eyes. The raw edge of the binding should meet the raw edge of the quilt top exactly.

As you approach the corner, stop exactly ⅜" from the edge of the quilt. It will be difficult to see this because the binding will be in the way. A marked line may help. Backstitch, and take the quilt out of the machine.

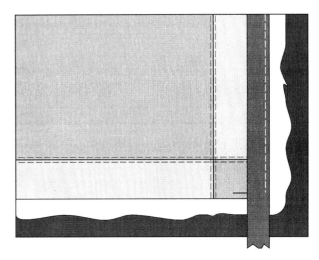

Stitch the binding to the quilt. Stop ⅜" from the corner.

Turn the quilt to the next side. Fold the binding so that the raw edges are again lined up with the raw edge of the quilt top. Bring the fold up to the edge of the quilt top on the side you just stitched. Stitch the second side.

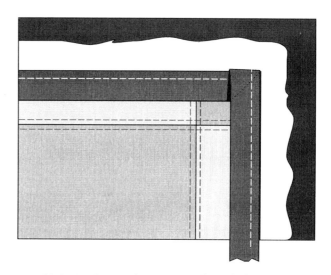

Fold the binding at the corner and stitch the next side.

Stitch the rest of the binding, stopping about 6" from the beginning. Take the quilt out of the machine, and lay it on a flat surface.

Unfold the ends of the binding as far back towards the stitching line as possible while keeping the bottom edge even with the edge of the quilt top. Lay the left tail over the right tail.

Mark a guideline on the right tail at the exact point where the left tail meets it, closest to the edge of the quilt top.

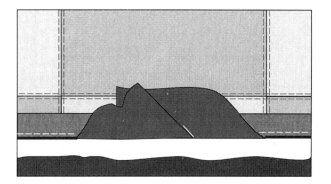

Mark a guideline at the end of the binding.

Use the marked line to draw a 45° angle exactly ½" from the edge of the *left* of the mark. Use a rotary ruler and the angled cut end as a guide.

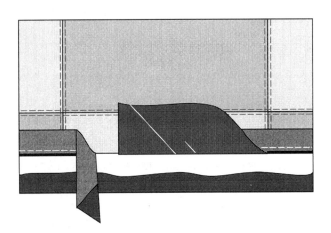

Mark a cutting line exactly ½" to the left of the guideline.

Cut the right tail on the marked line. Bunch up the quilt, and pin the two ends of the binding, right sides together. It will feel a little like wrestling an alligator, but that's only temporary. Stitch the binding with a ¼" seam. Press the seam allowance to one side with the very tip of your iron, which is about all you'll be able to get in there, and refold the binding. Sew the last section of the binding to the quilt.

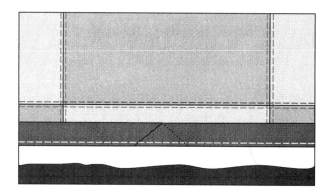

Sew the last part of the binding to the quilt.

If the binding will be turned to the back and stitched by hand, trim the batting and lining close to the quilt top. If it will be stitched by machine, a little more clearance is needed, so trim them even with the quilt top.

The slickest way I've ever seen to machine stitch a binding comes from Nancy Jacoby of Wabash, Indiana. She brings the edge of the binding to the back of the quilt so that it covers the stitching line by about ⅛". Then she pins it from the *top* and stitches "in the ditch," directly on the seam line between the binding and the border. All the pins must face the same direction, with their heads away from the needle. That way they can be yanked out in the nick of time just before the needle attempts to sew through them.

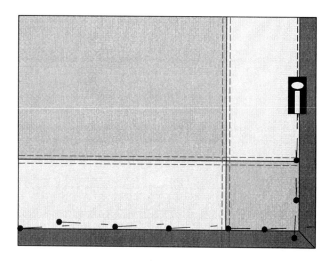

Bring the binding to the back of the quilt and pin from the top to finish the binding by machine.

Gallery Of Quilts

"Mom's Wedding Day" (right) by Terry J. Blitchok of Lake Orion, Michigan, is a beautiful tribute to her mother, Sarah Dennis. A single photo-transfer of her mother, wearing the wedding gown she made, is set in a frame of four complementary print fabrics along with a handful of black scraps.

The Album *block is a great gift for a bride, a graduate, or anyone celebrating a very special occasion. It can also be made into a cover for a ring binder to hold wedding pictures or special mementos. (See pages 42 and 43.)*

"Heart & Flowers" (below) was made by Lucy A. Fazely and Terri Lamrock. It features pictures of Terri and her family in a Watercolor *quilt. Photos were chosen by how well they blended with neighboring fabrics. Lucy and Terri placed them randomly throughout the bottom of the quilt for a beautifully subtle effect. (See page 41.)*

When my assistant, Teresa, began working for me back in 1992, she thought one of the perks of the job would be learning how to quilt. Well, she hit the ground running and I'm ashamed to say we haven't found the time to have our first quilting lesson yet!

Since "Cute As A Button" features photographs of Teresa's three children, she'll at least be getting a quilt out of the deal! Her daughter, Jenny, is shown at left posing with a snowman.

Cloth-covered buttons help tie the bold colors of this quilt together, as does the variegated thread in the "scribble" quilting motif. This pattern of twirling triangles is called Whirligig. *(See page 44.)*

The readers of my on-line newsletter came to my rescue by sending me their best family photographs when I had depleted my own stash of snapshots. "Let Me Have Your Best Shot" is the happy result of their generosity.

The photo-transfers of children, grandchildren and special pets are framed by strips of bright colored fabric and three-dimensional triangles made from folded squares of black cloth.

Quilting lines form a box within each block. The quilted box is then repeated in the sashing strips. Additional quilting lines run diagonally through the folded triangles, crisscrossing through the set squares. Prairie points take the place of a traditional applied binding. This original design is called Snapshot. (See page 46.)

What child could resist a teddy bear or other stuffed toy with pictures of themselves and their friends stitched right in? These cuddly toys were made by piecing photo-transfers and sashing strips together to create patchwork just slightly larger than the pattern piece. Then the patchwork was cut, as if it were regular fabric, and assembled following pattern directions. These bears were originally made for Woman's Day *magazine and appeared in the March 4, 1997 issue. (See page 49.)*

"Drewie & Bessie" by Linda Kay Bodker of Clarkston, Michigan, is a look back at those sweet, delicious years when the children were young and Mom and Dad had all the answers. Photos of children climbing trees, blowing bubbles and playing at the beach make Variable Star *the perfect block to showcase family memories. (See page 50.) Expand the block with another set of star points and create a companion tote bag. (See* Star Within A Star Tote Bag *on page 52.)*

"Boys & Their Toys" by Sue DeWitt of Fenton, Michigan, is about her men and their machines. Husband Barry, son Kevin, and nephew Anthony mugged for the camera astride bicycles, motorcycles and dirt bikes. They posed with shiny new cars, vintage autos, and old clunkers. They had their pictures taken piloting everything from race cars to lawn mowers, snow-mobiles to remote controlled toy cars. There is even a picture showing the results of a race car that had a bad day at the track! Each photo-transfer is framed in a traditional set of Snowballs & Nine Patches, and the whole quilt is bordered in race car fabric. (See page 56.) On the back of the quilt (right) is the lone girl and her toy: a red 'Vette!

"Gone Fishin" by Lucy A. Fazely (above) features photo-transfers of her son, Jeremy, near their Oscoda, Michigan, home. The biggest fish so far? The 3½ pound bass in the bottom picture.

Stacked Snowballs is the perfect block with which to brag about your sportsman, scholar, or athlete. (See page 55.)

Lucy's design was first published in Quick & Easy Quilting, August 1998.

Eight close friends meet weekly to stitch quilts and share their lives. They call themselves *The Hen Gang*. Patsy Hartz of Oxford, Michigan, made this little quilt (right) in their honor. *"Circle of Friends"* features a photo-transfer of each member, plus group shots, and a picture of their rubber chicken mascot reclining on a shelf loaded with fabric.

Clear solid colors and an unexpected quilting motif direct attention to the photo-transfers in this Square Within A Square. *(See page 58.)*

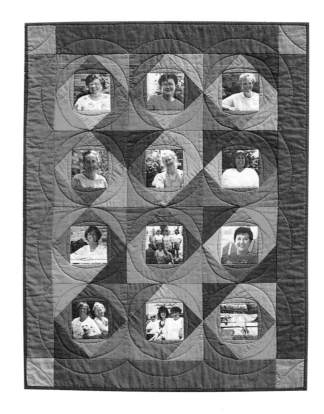

Mary Lynn Andrews of Grand Blanc, Michigan, got the inspiration for this quilt while sitting in the waiting room of her optometrist's office. She decided to collect pictures of kids wearing glasses for a quilt called "The Eyes Have It" (left). *Mary's choice of vibrant, playful colors was a great match for this traditional* Counterpane *block. (See page 60.)*

Mary took the same quilt block and made matching patchwork to decorate a sheet set she calls "Sweet Dreams" (above left). *Just about any of the blocks in this book can be used to make patchwork hems on sheets and pillowcases to tie bedding and wall quilts together in a common theme. (See page 62.)*

Jennie Simms and Pamela McCarthy have been best friends since early pre-K. Our two families have grown very close, too. "Family Fotos" features selected snapshots from the McCarthy family photo albums in bright yellow stars on a field of blue.

After laying the finished blocks out on the floor to see where they should be placed in the quilt, I noticed to my horror that the color scheme I had chosen was very nearly maize and blue. The McCarthys are ardent Michigan State University fans and I certainly couldn't give them a quilt that even remotely resembled the school colors of the University of Michigan, their arch rival! I quickly added the lime green sashing strips and bright red set squares to the Pinwheel Star blocks so the quilt wouldn't have any resemblance to U of M colors. Go GREEN?! (See page 64.)

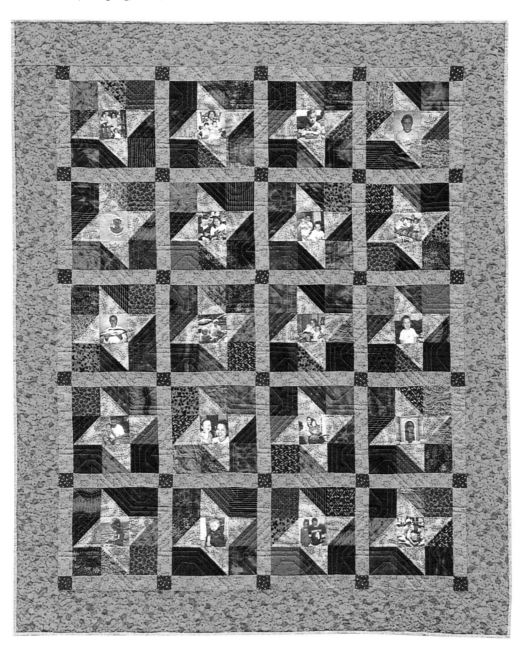

"Shutterbugs" is the second quilt made with a whole lot of pictures of people I don't even know! Newsletter readers responded to my SOS for photographs so enthusiastically there were enough for two quilts! (I only had to add one or two family members and a couple friends.)

The photo-transfers sit askew in blocks that twist, called Spinning Windmill. (Not recommended for quilters who suffer from vertigo!) The blocks are framed with sashing strips in a wild red print, and set squares "fussy-cut" from polka dot fabric. Appliqued circles or cloth-covered buttons would have worked too, but this was much faster. (See page 74.)

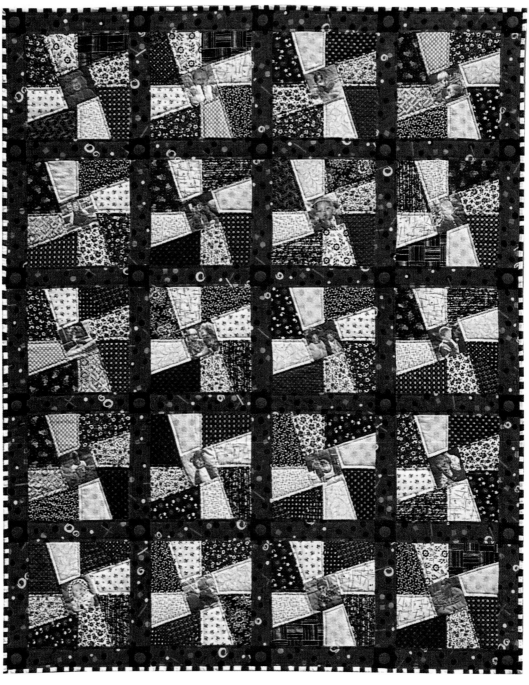

Plain white cloth mouse pads and coasters accept photo-transfers beautifully and make wonderful quick gifts when you're in a hurry. Besides, they're really fun to do. Make some for yourself, too. Put pictures of your kids, grandkids or vacation snapshots on them. (See page 63 for instructions, and Resources, page 77, for ordering information.)

Sophie Crittenden from Mansfield, Ohio, came up with another quick project that looks terrific. She took a man's vest that she found at a thrift store for 50¢ and machine appliqued black and white photo-transfers above the pockets for a very wearable garment.

Overlapping the photo-transfers and placing them at odd angles is what makes the idea really work. Another option would be to embellish the photo-transfers, or other areas of the vest, with lace. (See page 63.)

Don't forget that a color photograph can be turned into a black and white photo-transfer when the transfer is made on the color copier.

Sharon Castle of Falcon Heights, Minnesota, created this extraordinary quilt called "House Full of Memories" for her in-laws' 20th wedding anniversary. By time the quilt was completed, a move was underway from Minnesota to Oregon and the pictorial quilt of the home they were now leaving took on an even more special meaning.

The recipients of the quilt are pictured standing in the driveway. Grandparents, children, grandchildren and all kinds of kin are in the windows, behind doors, and surrounding the quilt. The tree above the garage, the cloud, the front door and a window all "open" to reveal yet another family member.

Peel-and-stick word balloons with appropriate sayings were added to some pictures before they were transferred. Sharon transferred both black and white photographs and color photographs to beige fabric using sepia tones. This was done with a special option she selected on a Canon color copier to give the photo-transfers an old-fashioned look.

After the pictures were transferred, Sharon left about ¼" of fabric showing around the edges of each transfer in the border and wrote captions with permanent fabric pen, as if they were going into a real scrapbook. The photo-transfers were then fused to the border fabric using paper-backed fusible web and "secured" with squares of dark green fabric folded diagonally. The raw edges were finished with a blanket stitch. (No pattern given.)

Doilies made with crocheted lace or Battenburg lace on fabric show off photo-transfers to perfection. Use them as Christmas tree ornaments, lapel pins, or to embellish the top of a pillow.

The doily's fabric insert is too coarse to transfer on, so use a 200 thread count white cotton to transfer on instead. Satin stitch with matching or contrasting thread to cover raw edges and this project will take but a minute. For those items like tree ornaments that won't be laundered, glitter is fun. (See page 63.) The lace pillow was originally made for Woman's Day magazine and appeared in the May 12, 1998 issue.

Wedding Pillow photos courtesy Marty Abrin, Photo Video Center, Southfield, MI.

The three vests pictured here were made by Gina Angell of Duxbury, Massachusetts. The photo-transfers were puzzled together with sashing strips, then cut from a commercial vest pattern.

The vest on the left was made for Gina's friend, Eileen, using photographs of Eileen's husband and grandchildren. One patch has the message: "I love you grandma from Kyla and Zack."

Gina made the vest in the middle for herself using photographs of her family. The little vest at the right was made for her 4-year-old son, Jason, who is pictured with his father. (See page 49.)

This Hole In The Barn Door *quilt was made by Terry J. Blitchok of Lake Orion, Michigan. It is called "The Men In My Life" and was made in memory of several of Terry's male relatives who passed away recently. It's also a family tree of sorts with photo-transfers of Terry's grandparents, father, father-in-law, husband, sons and nephews. (See page 66.)*

Phidge Olds Sweers of Goodrich, Michigan, created "In Pursuit" using family photographs and a two-block Log Cabin in warm, fuzzy flannels.

Made for her husband, Carl, it includes photographs of hunting expeditions, golf outings, fishing trips, and choice snapshots of son Erik. (See page 68.)

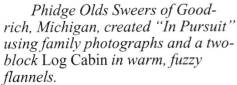

Stitched to the back of the quilt is Phidge's signature label, above. It includes a photo of her and Carl at a costume party. The photo-transfer of the two 50s kids was silhouetted, and then fused with paper-backed fusible web to the striped fabric of the label. Information about the quilt was written directly onto the fabric label with a permanent pen.

Sisters Sophie Crittenden and Mary Ellen Wojcik from Mansfield, Ohio, brought their creative talents together to make these three photo-transfer neckties. Photographs from a vacation to Arizona and a birthday were taken with a disposable panoramic camera in the vertical format. The collage of cats was made with standard sized photos. (See page 49.)

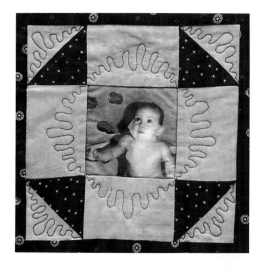

Kathy Bradbury's Shoo Fly quilt is called "Don't Fly Away." It's made with photographs of her daughter, Bobbi. The pictures she chose to transfer include snapshots of Bobbi at all different ages, capturing the special moments in her life. Notice the unusual quilting motif that fills the lighter spaces so well. (See page 70.)

Photo Quilt Blocks™ are the no-sew alternative to very small wall quilts. Photo-transfers and fabric are punched into a 12" foam block with a butter knife. They call for a single photo-transfer in the middle, but the kit contains enough supplies to include more. I made this one using photo-transfers of my husband and daughter. (See Resources.)

School pictures are framed with red ribbon in "School Days," a denim Trip Around The World, *originally featured in the* August 4, 1998 *issue of* Woman's Day *magazine. Waistbands and back patch pockets from the recycled jeans add interest and a special place for bandannas or small treasures. (See page 54.)*

Shana, Noah, and Reeves are "Kathleen's Kidlets," and my niece and nephews. Their quilt, a Log Window, is a cross between a Log Cabin and an Attic Window. No matter what the name, it's fast and fun to put together. (See page 72.)

To get the most out of this pattern, use photographs that have a light background, like this one of Reeves. It gives the illusion of greater depth.

The Patterns

Small photo-transfers hidden among the floral patches offer unexpected surprises in this simple one-patch. A single heart among the flowers adds a dramatic focal point. (See page 25.)
Quilt size: 30" x 24" • Finished block: 1½" • Finished photo-transfer: 1½" • Transfer paper: 2-5 sheets

1. Trim photo-transfers to 2" x 2 ".

2. Cut 2" strips from each of at least 15 different large floral prints selected for their variety, color and value. Cut these strips into 2" squares. A total of 192 fabric squares and photo-transfers will be needed.

3. Using a design wall or large flat surface, audition patches and photo-transfers. Study the color photograph of "Heart & Flowers" on page 25 for inspiration.

4. Join patches together. Cut two pieces 3" x 24½" for top and bottom borders and two pieces 3" x 23½" for side borders (about ½ yd.). Add top and bottom borders first, then side borders. Cut lining 34" x 28" (1 yd.). To bind, join 3 strips of 2½" wide fabric (¼ yd.).

Quilting Suggestion:
Meander through the posies in a serpentine path, stopping to outline a petal here or a flower there. Let the fabric be your guide.

Album

*Quilt size: about 16" x 18", depending on
the size of the photo-transfers.
Transfer paper: 1 sheet*

*Four ever-widening borders, punctuated with black triangles reminiscent of an old-fashioned photo
album, make an elegant setting for a single photograph. It's an easy project for a beginner and one that
will accommodate any size photo-transfer. (See page 25.)*

1. Begin with a large photo-transfer. Trim
   seam allowances to ¼".

2. Cut one strip from each of four different
   ¼ yard pieces of fabric in these widths:
   - Fabric A/B: 1"
   - Fabric C/D: 1½"
   - Fabric E/F: 2¼"
   - Fabric G/H: 2¾"

3. From a scrap of black fabric cut 4 squares
   in each of these dimensions: 1" x 1",
   1¼" x 1¼", 2" x 2", and 2½" x 2½".
   They will be triangles **#1**, **#2**, **#3**, and
   #4, respectively.

4. To make the block, stitch fabric **A/B**, cutting strips to fit. Press seam allowances
   towards strips. Place **#1** squares on
   corners, sew diagonally, and trim to ¼".

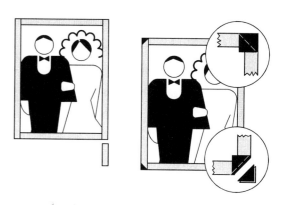

5. Repeat with remaining 3 fabrics and corresponding black squares.

Photo Album Cover

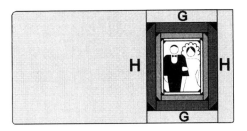

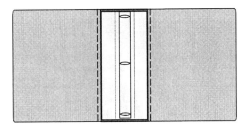

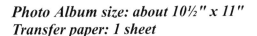

Photo Album size: about 10½" x 11"
Transfer paper: 1 sheet

*Create a striking quilted cover for any size album using essentially the same layout as the previous pattern. Note that the smallest size triangles are repeated to frame the photo-transfer before any strips are added, and the largest triangles have been omitted. Also, a total of ¾ yard **G/H** fabric is required.*

1. With a suitably sized photo-transfer, create the block. (See page 42.) Center it on binder's front cover to check size. Increase width of **G** and **H** so patchwork measures at least 1" larger on all sides than binder when is opened flat. Fuse wrong side of quilt top to fusible fleece. Add backing, quilt, and trim all layers to ¾" larger than binder.

2. Cut three rectangles 10" wide and as tall as the height of the album cover. Stitch ¼" hems as shown.

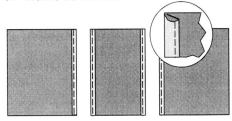

3. Position right side of hemmed rectangles on right side of quilt top as shown, raw edges even. Center last rectangle as shown. Stitch ¼" from raw edge. Turn right side out. Insert binder.

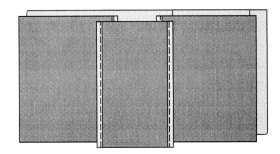

Whirligig

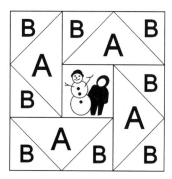

Four triangles encircle each photo-transfer in this whimsical quilt framed by sashing strips and set squares. Self-covered buttons sewn in each set square provide a delightful accent. (See page 26.)
Quilt size: 55" x 65" • Finished block: 9" • Finished photo-transfer: 3" • Transfer paper: 4 sheets

CUTTING CHART

Patch/Sashing/Border	Quantity	Dimension		Strip Width	No. of Strips	Yield / Strip	Yards
Photo-transfer	20	3½" x 3½"		—	—	—	1
A	80	3½" x 6½"		3½"	20	4	2
B	160	3½" x 3½"		3½"	20	8	2
Sashing Strips	49	2" x 9½"		2"	13	4	⅞
Set Squares	30	2" x 2"		2"	2	20	¼
Inner Border	2, 2	44"	56½"	1½"	5	—	¼
Middle Border	2, 2	46"	57½"	1"	5	—	¼
Outer Border	2, 2	47"	65"	4¼"	8	—	1⅛
Lining	2	35" x 59"		—	—	—	3⅓
Binding	1	2½" x 250"		2½"	7	—	⅝

1. Place one **B** on **A** and stitch diagonally as shown. Trim to ¼" and press towards **B**. Repeat for other **B**.

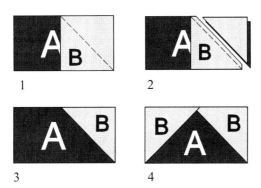

2. Partially stitch first **B-A-B** unit to photo-transfer as shown. Working counter-clockwise around photo-transfer, sew the next **B-A-B** unit. Press seam allowances away from the photo-transfer.

3. Continue by adding the third **B-A-B** unit.

4. Add the last **B-A-B** unit and finish stitching the first seam to complete the block.

5. Join blocks, sashing strips and set squares. Add borders.

Quilting Suggestion:
*Try "scribble quilting" with variegated rayon thread for a different look in the large, dark **A** triangles. A continuous line of more traditional echo quilting ¼" from the seam is a nice accompaniment.*

With both methods, travel from one triangle to the next by stitching "in the ditch," or seam line.

Snapshot

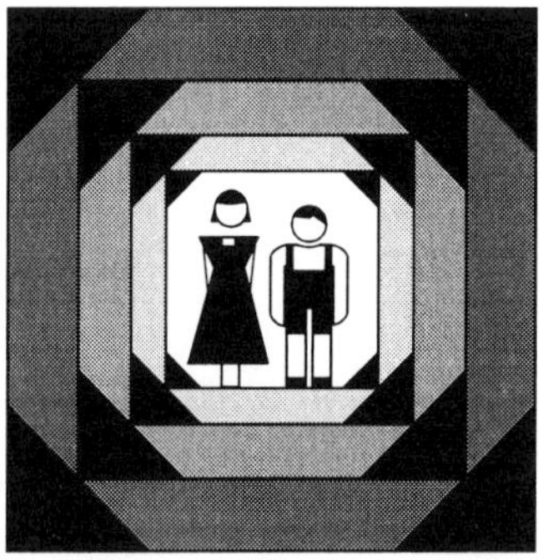

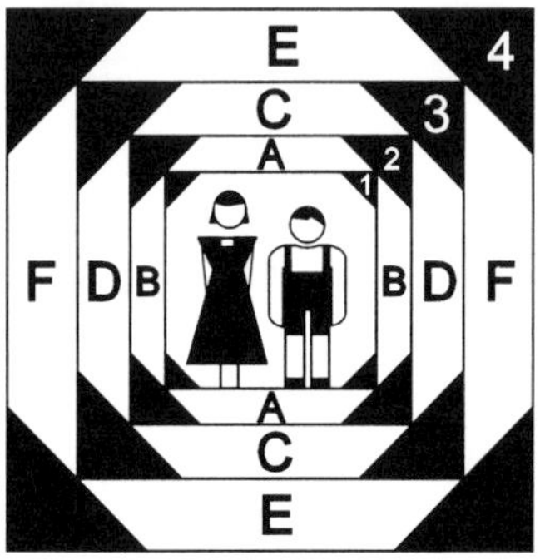

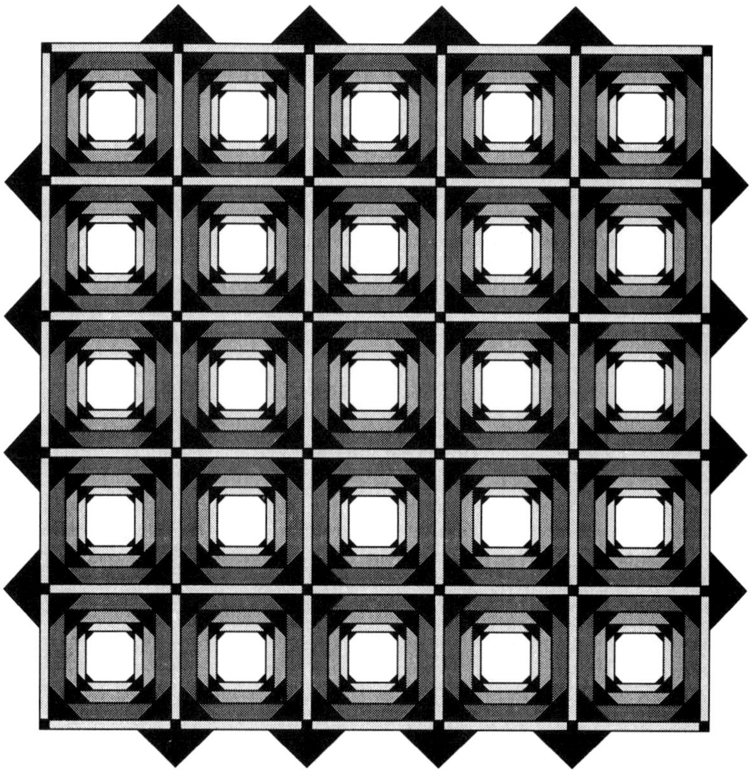

Three-dimensional black triangles made from folded squares give this quilt extra pizzazz and a fun place to stick inquisitive fingers. It's constructed like a Log Cabin *with the triangles slipped in the seams to camouflage the ends of the "logs." Prairie points add to the fun. (See page 27.)*

Quilt size: 41" x 41" • Finished block: 7½" • Finished photo-transfer: 3" • Transfer paper: 5 sheets

CUTTING CHART

Patch/Sashing/Border	Quantity	Dimension	Strip Width	No. of Strips	Yield / Strip	Yards
Photo-transfer	25	3½" x 3½"	—	—	—	1
A	50	1" x 3½"	1"	7	8	½
B	50	1" x 4½"	1"	7	8	
C	50	1¼" x 4½"	1¼"	7	8	¾
D	50	1¼" x 6"	1¼"	13	4	
E	50	1½" x 6"	1½"	13	4	1¼
F	50	1½" x 8"	1½"	13	4	
Folded Triangles #1	100	1" x 1"	1"	3	36	1½
Folded Triangles #2	100	1½" x 1½"	1½"	5	24	
Folded Triangles #3	100	2" x 2"	2"	7	16	
Folded Triangles #4	100	2½" x 2½"	2½"	9	12	
Sashing Strips	60	1" x 8"	1"	15	4	½
Set Squares	36	1" x 1"	1"	1	36	⅛
Prairie Points	16	5" x 5"	5"	2	8	⅓
Lining	1	44" x 44"	—	—	—	1⅓*

*If fabric width after laundering is less than 44", lining will need to be pieced. Double yardage.

1. Fold all squares (#1-#4) diagonally to make folded triangles. Press.

2. Position and pin all four **#1** triangles on the photo-transfer, with raw edges even. Sew **A** and **B** patches as shown, securing the triangles. Press seam allowances away from the photo-transfer.

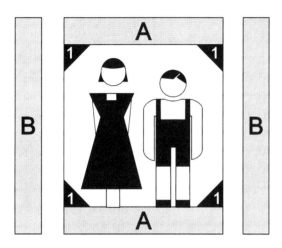

3. Position **#2** triangles. Pin in place. Stitch **C** and **D** as shown. Press as before.

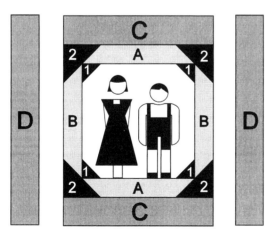

4. Position **#3** triangles. Stitch **E** and **F**. Press as before.

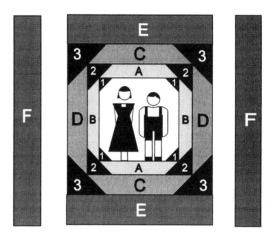

5. With raw edges even, baste **#4** triangles in each corner to complete block.

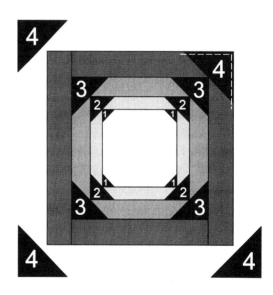

6. Join blocks, sashing strips and set squares.

7. To make prairie points, fold 5" squares in half. Press. Bring upper corners down to middle of bottom. Press. Baste.

8. Position prairie points face down on finished quilt top, centering slits over set squares, even with raw edges. Baste.

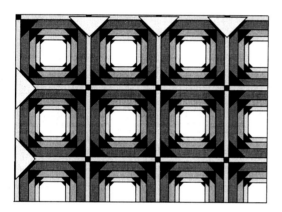

9. Press completed quilt top. Fuse wrong side of quilt top to fusible fleece according to instructions. (See Resources.) Trim fleece to meet raw edges of quilt top exactly.

10. Pin quilt top to quilt lining, right sides together.

11. With a ¼" seam allowance, stitch top to lining. Leave about a 12" opening. Trim backing to meet top.

12. Turn quilt right-side out. Slip stitch opening. Pull out prairie points. Press. Baste ½" from edge, in preparation for quilting.

Quilting Suggestion:

*Quilt through the center of **F** patches gently lifting the #4 folded triangles to hide the beginnings and endings of the quilting thread.*

Then quilt diagonally from the corners of the photo-transfer patch through the folded triangles toward the set square. Continue quilting through the set square and then on into the folded triangles of the next block.

Photo-Transfer Teddy Bears & Vests

Any pattern piece without darts, pleats, folds or tucks can include photo-transfers, be it a pattern for a teddy bear, vest, or other type of garment. (See pages 28 and 36.) Decide in which area to incorporate the photo-transfers and locate the corresponding pattern piece. Establish which is the "right" side, and which side is right-side-up. Knowing how the pattern piece fits in the scheme of things is essential, otherwise, your photo-transfers could accidentally be stitched upside-down, or worse yet, *inside* the bear!

Audition photographs on top of the pattern piece with at least 1" space between them. Decide which can be transferred as is, which need to be enlarged or reduced, and which aren't really needed. Once the images are transferred, trim them to a scant quarter inch.

Then cut a variety of different fabrics into 1½" strips: wider if the area is big, narrower if the area is small. Sash the photo-transfers with the strips of fabric. This technique is explored much more fully in my book, *Creating Scrapbook Quilts*. (See Resources.) Add fabric strips and photo-transfers until the patchwork is about an inch larger than the pattern piece on all sides.

Some photographs may be cut off in a seam line. If that doesn't appeal, position them more towards the center and add additional fabric strips on the outside.

It is easiest to build the patchwork in strips, either vertically or horizontally. Since seam allowances will "shrink" the photo-transfers and fabric strips, lay the pattern piece on top of the patchwork from time to time to check the size.

Another way to check progress is to make a window template. Trace the seam lines onto a piece of tag board at least 1" larger than the pattern piece. Cut on the traced seam lines to create a hole or window. Place the patchwork under the window template to see exactly how much will be visible once the seams are sewn.

When the patchwork is complete, lay the pattern piece on top as you normally would and cut out the pattern. Assemble the project following the pattern directions.

Two of the vests made by Gina Angell were from Carol Doak's book, *Easy Reversible Vests*. The third was from a ClothKits pattern. I made the 24" teddy bears from a DreamSpinners pattern. (See Resources, page 77.)

Photo-Transfer Neckties

Neckties are fun to embellish with photo-transfers. They can either be patched with sashing strips as described above, or made by ironing photo-transfers directly onto white fabric the size of the pattern piece, as Sophie Crittenden and her sister, Mary Ellen Wojcik, did.

Select one tall picture or arrange several photographs in a collage and copy them onto transfer paper. They may need to be enlarged or reduced to fit properly.

It's a good idea to make a tag board template of that part of the tie that will show when worn. Remember, the image does not have to extend all the way to the seam line in this case, but it *must* go all the way across the front of the tie and beyond the fold to the back. (Getting the photo-transfer to end exactly on the fold of the tie on all four sides would be just too difficult.)

Transfer the images directly onto the necktie fabric. Remember to place the transfers on the *bias*, as that's how neckties need to be cut. Otherwise, they just won't hang right.

The ties shown on page 38 were made with Simplicity pattern #9345.

Variable Star

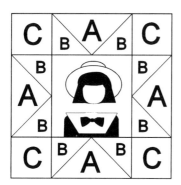

Shimmering stars in yellow and gold with photo-transfer centers rest on a background of blue.
Make each block a different color combination and put your scraps to good use. (See page 28.)
Quilt size: 25" x 31" • Finished block: 6" • Finished photo-transfer: 3" • Transfer paper: 2 sheets

CUTTING CHART

Patch/Sashing/Border	Quantity	Dimension		Strip Width	No. of Strips	Yield / Strip	Yards
Photo-transfer	12	3½" x 3½"		—	—	—	1
A	48	2" x 3½"		2"	6	8	½
B	96	2" x 2"		2"	5	20	⅓
C	48	2" x 2"		2"	3	20	¼
Inner Border	2, 2	18½"	25½"	1"	3	—	¼
Middle Border	2, 2	19½"	26"	¾"	3	—	⅛
Outer Border	2, 2	20"	30½"	2¾"	3	—	⅓
Lining	1	29" x 35"		—	—	—	1
Binding	1	2½" x 122"		2½"	4		⅓

1. Place **B** on **A** and stitch diagonally as shown. Trim seam allowance to ¼" and press towards **B**. Repeat for other **B**.

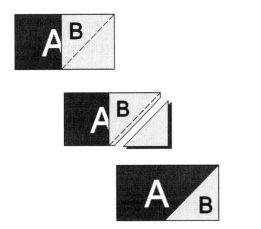

2. Stitch **B-A-B** units to photo-transfer, and **C** patches to **B-A-B** units as shown.

3. Join the three strips together to complete the block. Press seam allowances away from photo-transfer.

4. Join blocks and add borders.

Quilting Suggestion:

In addition to any other quilting you may wish to do, stitch "in the ditch" around each star. Then quilt through the A and C patches as shown in one long continuous line, quilting in the ditch to get from one patch to the next.

Star Within A Star Tote Bag

This handy, lined tote becomes a brag bag with the addition of a special photograph, centered in the star. Two blocks, one on either side, double the fun. (See page 28.)

Tote size: 16" x 17" • Finished photo-transfer: 4" • Transfer paper: 1 sheet

CUTTING CHART

Patch/Sashing/Border	Quantity	Dimension	Strip Width	No. of Strips	Yield / Strip	Yards
Photo-transfer	1	4½" x 4½"	—	—	—	1
A	4	2½" x 4½"	2½"	1	8	⅛
B	8	2½" x 2½"	2½"	1	16	⅛
C	4	2½" x 2½"	2½"	1	16	⅛
D	4	4½" x 8½"	4½"	1	4	¼
E	8	4½" x 4½"	4½"	1	8	¼
F	4	4½" x 4½"	4½"	1	8	¼
Lining	1	16½" x 32½"	16½"	1	1	½
Handles	2	1½" x 15"	1½"	1	2	⅛
Band/Facing	1	2½" x 32½"	2½"	1	1	⅛

1. Follow directions on page 51 for Variable Star, adding patches **D**, **E**, and **F** to make two 16" blocks. Quilt each one. With right sides together, stitch sides and bottom of tote. Turn right side out.

2. Fold short sides of lining piece together, right sides touching. Stitch as shown to make a pocket. Tuck into tote and pin even with top edges of tote.

3. To make handles, fuse 1" strip of fusible fleece to wrong side of each handle as shown, ¼" from short sides and ¼" from top. Then with right sides together, seam long sides and carefully turn right side out. Press and topstitch.

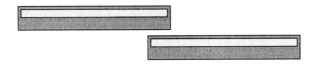

4. Fuse 1" strip fusible fleece to wrong side of band/facing, as in step #3 for handles. With right sides together, stitch short sides.

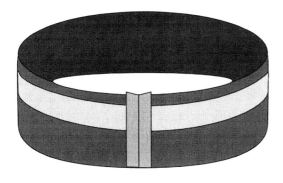

5. Place band/facing over tote opening as shown. Re-pin, catching band/facing, tote and lining. Slip handles in position inside tote against lining. Stitch through all layers: band/facing, tote, lining, handles.

6. Turn facing under ¼", pin fold at stitching line inside tote, and slipstitch. To finish, flip the handles up and stitch to band/facing.

Trip Around The World

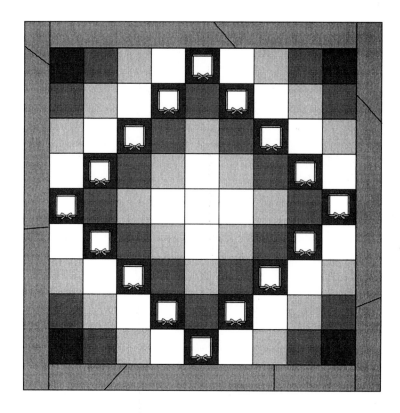

Six pairs of recycled denim jeans in four color gradations from light to dark form the backdrop for 16 school pictures trimmed in approximately 8 yards of ¼" red ribbon. Approximately 1¾ yards of lining fabric is required. (See page 39.)

Quilt size: 57" x 57" • Finished block: 5½" • Finished photo-transfer: 2½" x 2½" • Transfer paper: 2 sheets

1. Carefully remove back pockets and waist bands. Cut fronts and backs apart close to seams to salvage the most denim. Cut 20 6"x 6" patches from each of the 4 colors, and 1 extra from the lightest. (Baste front pockets shut before cutting.) Cut 2 borders 4" x 50" and 2 borders 4" x 57" piecing denim as needed to reach desired size.

2. Assemble patches and borders as shown, piecing border pieces in any way possible to reach desired size.

3. Trim photo-transfers to 2½" x 2½". (The image must reach all the way to the edge of the photo-transfer.) Center photo-transfers in the darkest patches.

4. Place ribbon over raw edges and zigzag in place. (Fold ribbon at corners. Overlap end over end to finish. Tack on bow.)

5. Whipstitch two 1¾ yd pieces of fusible fleece together, then fuse it to back of quilt top. Trim fleece to meet quilt top. Cut backing fabric 2" larger than quilt on all sides, piecing if necessary. With right sides together, stitch ¼" from edge, leaving 12" opening along center side. Trim backing to meet top. Turn right-side out. Press. Slipstitch opening.

Quilting Suggestion:
With matching thread, quilt through ribbon. If desired, quilt diagonally through the other patches or "in the ditch."

Stacked Snowballs

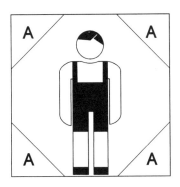

Stacked Snowballs is the perfect project for a beginner. Using just three photo-transfers and two fabrics (¼ yard dark, ⅝ yard light), it can be assembled and quilted in just a few hours. (See page 29.)
Quilt size: 9" x 18" • Finished block: 4" • Finished photo-transfer: 4" • Transfer paper: 1-2 sheets

1. Trim photo-transfers to 4½" x 4½". Cut 12 **A** squares 1¾" x 1¾" from dark fabric.

2. Place one **A** on each corner of the photo-transfer. Sew diagonally. Trim seam allowances to ¼". Press towards corners.

3. From the same dark fabric cut:
   4 sashing strips 1" x 4½"
   2 sashing strips 1" x 16"
   2 strips 2½" wide for binding

4. From a different (light) fabric cut:
   2 border pieces 2" x 5½"
   2 border pieces 2" x 19"
   1 lining 13" x 22"

5. Join blocks and sashing strips. Add borders.

Snowballs & Nine Patches

#1

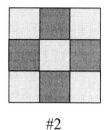

#2

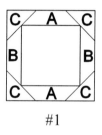

#1

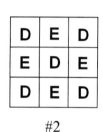

#2

Eighteen Snowball blocks and 17 Nine Patch blocks are combined to make this beautiful traditional quilt. It's a perfect place to show off family photographs. Keep the color strategy simple and tie it all together with a novelty print appropriate to the theme of the quilt. (See page 29.)

Quilt size: 30" x 39" • Finished block: 4½" • Finished photo-transfer : 3" • Transfer paper: 3 sheets

CUTTING CHART

Patch/Sashing/Border	Quantity	Dimension		Strip Width	No. of Strips	Yield / Strip	Yards
Photo-transfer	18	3½" x 3½"		—	—	—	1
A	36	1¼" x 3½"		1¼"	5	8	¼
B	36	1¼" x 5"		1¼"	5	8	¼
C	72	2" x 2"		2"	4	20	⅓
D	85	2" x 2"		2"	5	20	⅓
E	68	2" x 2"		2"	4	20	⅓
Inner Border	2, 2	23"	32½"	¾"	4	—	⅛
Outer Border	2, 2	23½"	38½"	3½"	4	—	½
Lining	1	34" x 43"		—	—	—	1¼
Binding	1	2½" x 148"		2½"	5	—	½

1. Stitch **A**, then **B** as shown. Press seam allowances away from photo-transfer.

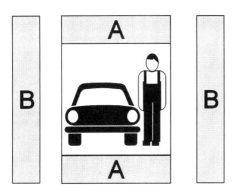

2. Place one **C** on each corner, raw edges even. Sew diagonally. Trim seam allowances and press towards corners to complete the block. Make 18 blocks.

3. Join **D** and **E** patches as shown. Press seam allowances towards **E** patches.

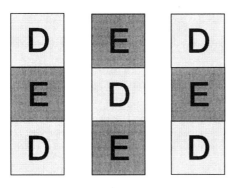

4. Join the two **D-E-D** strips to the **E-D-E** strip to complete the block. Press seam allowances towards **E-D-E**. Make 17 blocks.

5. Join blocks according to the diagram. Add borders.

Quilting Suggestions:

First, quilt an overall grid pattern by stitching diagonally through the Nine Patch blocks. Move from one to the other in a continuous line of quilting from border to border.

Then quilt a box around the photo-transfer by stitching through the center of each A and B patch. Move from A to B by stitching diagonally "in the ditch" (on the seam line) along the long side of patch C.

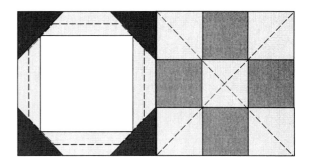

Square Within A Square

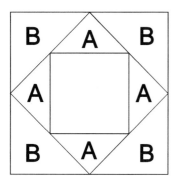

This old standby hardly seems the same with a photo-transfer in the center. The variety of "lights" and "darks" adds still more interest, and the circular quilting motif provides an excellent contrast to the straight seam lines, making this quilt anything but ordinary. (See page 30.)

Quilt size: 22" x 28" • Finished block: 6" • Finished photo-transfer: 3" • Transfer paper: 2 sheets

CUTTING CHART

Patch/Sashing/Border	Quantity	Dimension		Strip Width	No. of Strips	Yield / Strip	Yards
Photo-transfer	12	3½" x 3½"		—	—	—	1
A	12	4¼" x 4¼"		4¼"	2	8	⅓
B	24	3⅞" x 3⅞"		3⅞"	3	8	½
Corner Squares	4	2¼" x 2¼"		2¼"	1	16	⅛
Border	2, 2	18½"	24½"	2¼"	3	—	¼
Lining	1	26" x 32"		—	—	—	1
Binding	1	2½" x 110"		2½"	3	—	¼

1. Cut **A** squares diagonally twice to make quarter-square triangles. Cut **B** squares diagonally once to make half-square triangles.

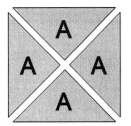 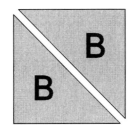

2. Center and stitch **A** patches on photo-transfers. (Note: the corners of **A** will extend beyond the sides of the photo-transfer, hence the need to center them.) Press seam allowances towards **A**.

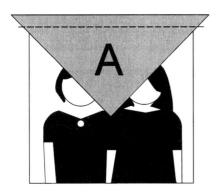

3. Center and stitch **B** patches as shown to complete block. (**B** patches will also need to be centered, as they will extend beyond the rest of the block.) Press seam allowances towards **B**.

4. Join blocks. Add borders and corner squares.

Quilting Suggestion:

Quilt shallow arcs through A triangles and slightly deeper arcs through B triangles. Continue the motif into the borders by quilting arcs the full width and length of each block. Quilt a reverse arc in each corner square.

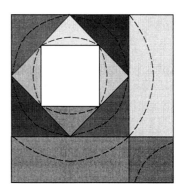

Counterpane

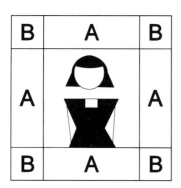

Alternating the value of the patches is the secret to making this simple pattern come alive. Make 12 dark blocks and 12 light blocks. Follow Mary's inspired color choices if you like and add an eye-catching inner border and colorful buttons to complete the quilt. (See page 30.)

Quilt size: 27" x 37" • Finished block: 5" • Finished photo-transfer: 3" • Transfer paper: 4 sheets

CUTTING CHART

Patch/Sashing/Border	Quantity	Dimension		Strip Width	No. of Strips	Yield / Strip	Yards
Photo-transfer	24	3½" x 3½"		—	—	—	1
A (light)	48	1½" x 3½"		1½"	6	8	⅓
B (dark)	48	1½" x 1½"		1½"	2	24	⅛
A (dark)	48	1½" x 3½"		1½"	6	8	⅓
B (light)	48	1½" x 1½"		1½"	2	24	⅛
Inner Border	2, 2	20½"	32½"	1½"	4	—	¼
Outer Border	2, 2	22½"	36½"	2½"	4	—	⅓
Lining	1	31" x 41"		—	—	—	1
Binding	1	2½" x 138"		2½"	4	—	⅓

1. Make 12 blocks with *light* rectangles and *dark* squares. Join patches as shown. Press seam allowances towards **A** in the center strip and towards **A** in the two side strips. Join the three strips together. Press seam allowances towards **B-A-B** strips.

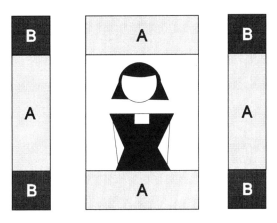

2. Make 12 blocks with *dark* rectangles and *light* squares. Join patches as shown. Press seam allowances towards **A** in the center strip and towards **A** in thc two side strips. Join the three strips together. Press seam allowances towards **B-A-B** strips.

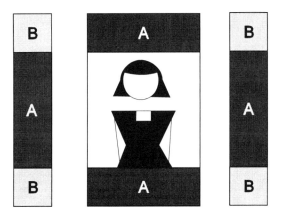

3. Join blocks and add borders to complete the quilt top.

Quilting Suggestion:

For fewer starts and stops, stitch long uninterrupted lines of quilting from one edge of the quilt to the other. Sew through the centers of the squares and rectangles to make a simple, yet effective grid pattern. Bright colored thread, instead of matching or neutral thread, is a great choice for bold fabrics.

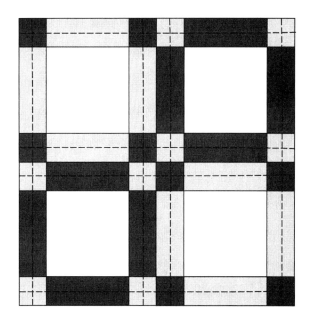

Counterpane Sheets & Pillowcases

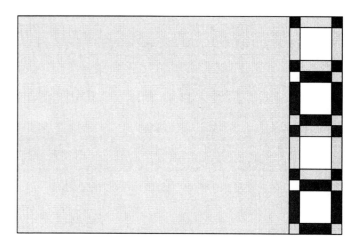

Matching sheets and pillowcases are a great complement to any bed quilt or wall quilt. Just divide the width of the area that will hold the patchwork by the finished block width and add sashing strips at either end until the patchwork fits. No batting is required as no quilting is done. (See page 30.)

Finished block: 5" • Finished photo-transfer: 3" • Transfer paper: 4-9 sheets

1. Construct blocks needed using the directions on pages 60 and 61. A standard pillowcase will take up to 8 blocks (4 on each side) and a twin size top sheet will take 13. For other sizes:
    Full /2 pillowcases—32 blocks.
    Queen /2 pillowcases—34 blocks.
    King /4 pillowcases—53 blocks.
Since all sheets vary in size and few dimensions are equally divisible by 5" (finished block size), additional sashing strips may needed at each end so that the patchwork fits.

2. Select the proper orientation for the photo-transfers: sideways, or right-side-up. Either is acceptable for a pillowcase. For a sheet, the choice is to appreciate the photo-transfers while in the bed, or standing at the foot of it. Keep in mind that the sheet will be folded down over the blanket or quilt when the bed is made.

3. Join the blocks. Add sashing strips, if needed, to reach desired width. (For a pillowcase, stitch them into a tube the width of the finished pillowcase.)

4. Cut off the existing hem of the sheet or pillowcase through the stitching line. Use it to make a facing the same size as the patchwork strip.

5. With right sides together, join the patchwork strip to the sheet or pillowcase where the hem was. Press seam allowance towards the patchwork strip.

6. Then, with right sides together, sew the facing to the patchwork strip, leaving the bottom open. Fold under ¼" and whipstitch the facing to complete the project.

Mouse Pads & Coasters

All that is required is a white cloth mouse pad or coaster, and a picture copied to transfer paper in the appropriate dimensions. (See page 33 and Resources.) Size photographs so they extend beyond the edge of the mouse pad or coaster by at least ¼" on each side. This will provide something to grab onto when peeling the paper off, and will assure that the image will go all the way to the edge.

Put the mouse pad or coaster on a hard surface on the floor. I use an old piece of flat wood shelving protected by a piece of fabric. (Besides giving off a pretty disgusting odor when heated, the rubberized bottom can mark the wood. Also,

some of the image from the transfer paper hanging over the edge might get on the ironing surface.) Lay the transfer paper on top, and press with a hot iron as you would if making a transfer onto fabric.

After setting the iron down, grab a corner of the paper and peel it off. The corner of the mouse pad or coaster will come with it, so hold it down with a few layers of fabric or a dish towel wrapped around your finger. (Remember, it's HOT!) Don't hold the mouse pad or coaster down with a hard object (fingernail, scissors, pencil, ruler) as that might make a permanent indentation in the photo-transfer. (See page 33.)

Embellished Vest

Here's another quick and easy project, starting with a ready-made vest. (See page 33.) Select photographs, transfer them to fabric, and trim seam allowances to a scant ¼". Turn them under, position the photo-transfers on the garment, and either hand applique them in place or topstitch them with with nylon thread. Another option would be to use a decorative machine stitch or a blanket stitch.

Want a faster way? Transfer the photos to fabric and trim the photo-transfer to the *finished* size—without seam allowances. Using paper backed fusible web, fuse the photo-transfers directly to the vest. (See Resources.) Top stitching or decorative machine stitching would be appropriate to hold the photo-transfers in place if the garment will receive heavy use.

Lace Doily Ornaments

Battenburg and hand crocheted lace doily ornaments are easy to make with ready-made doilies (see Resources) and a photo-transfer sized to fit. (See page 35.)

Iron the photo-transfer onto 200 thread count white cotton and position it on the right side of the doily with a dab of fabric glue. (A pin will put an unsightly hole in the photo-transfer.)

From the *back,* stitch into the edge of the lace just past the fabric insert to hold the photo-transfer in place. Working from the back will ensure that the photo-transfer will fit the fabric insert exactly. Then, turn the doily to the right side and cut away the excess photo-transfer as close as possible to the line of stitching. Satin stitch over the raw edge.

Pinwheel Star

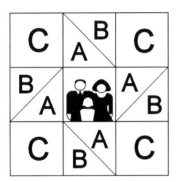

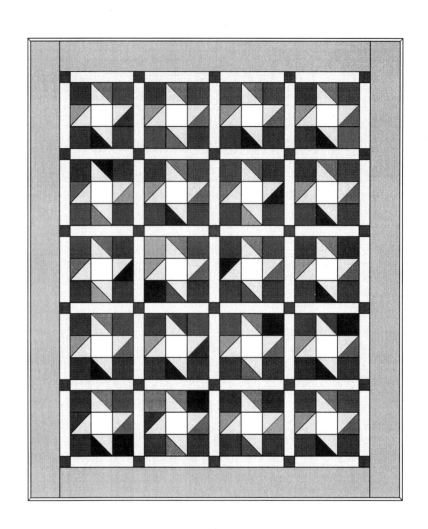

*Sparkling gold pinwheels slowly spinning on a field of blue provide 20 spaces for treasured photographs. Use many different fabrics for patches **B** and **C** to get a "scrappy" look. (See page 31.)*
Quilt size: 52" x 62" • Finished block: 9" • Finished photo-transfer: 3" • Transfer paper: 4 sheets

CUTTING CHART

Patch/Sashing/Border	Quantity	Dimension		Strip Width	No. of Strips	Yield / Strip	Yards
Photo-transfer	20	3½" x 3½"		—	—	—	1
A	80	3⅞" x 3⅞"		3⅞"	10	8	1¼
B	80	3⅞" x 3⅞"		3⅞"	10	8	1¼
C	80	3½" x 3½"		3½"	10	8	1⅛
Sashing Strips	49	2" x 9½"		2"	13	4	⅞
Set Squares	30	2" x 2"		2"	2	20	¼
Border	2, 2	43½"	62"	4¼"	6	—	¾
Lining	2	34" x 56"		—	—	—	3¼
Binding	1	2½" x 238"		2½"	7	—	⅝

1. Place **A** and **B** right sides together, raw edges even. Mark a diagonal line from corner to corner and stitch ¼" on both sides of the marked line. Cut on the line to yield two **A-B** triangle units. Press seam allowances towards **B**.

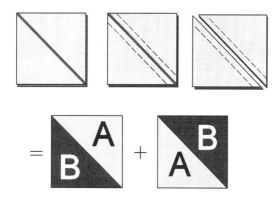

2. Stitch **A-B** triangle units to photo-transfer and to **C** patches as shown. Press seam allowances away from photo-transfer in the center strips, and towards **C** in the two side strips.

3. Join the three strips together to complete the block. Press seam allowances towards side strips.

4. Join blocks, sashing strips and set squares. Add borders.

Quilting Suggestion:

Use the side of your presser foot to "echo quilt" around the stars. Let the pattern extend into the sashing strips, stopping only when it meets the quilting lines from a neighboring block. Widths between quilting lines can be consistent or varied. Quilting lines can touch each other, cross over each other or have a cushion of visual space between them.

Try a light-colored thread for contrast.

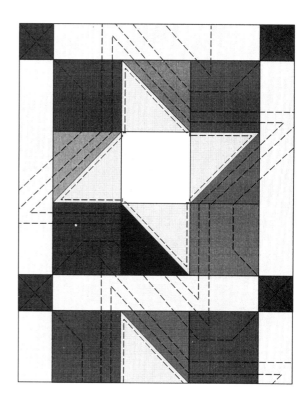

Hole In The Barn Door

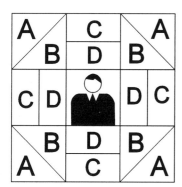

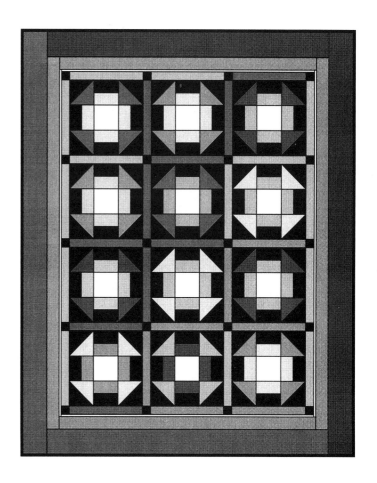

A large assortment of fabrics in Amish jewel-tone solids gives this quilt real character. See how the colors of the sashing strips and the borders vary, as do the triangles within the blocks. (See page 36.)
Quilt size: 41" x 51" • Finished block: 9" • Finished photo-transfer: 3" • Transfer paper: 2 sheets

CUTTING CHART

Patch/Sashing/Border	Quantity	Dimension		Strip Width	No. of Strips	Yield / Strip	Yards
Photo-transfer	12	3½" x 3½"		—	—	—	1
A	48	3⅞" x 3⅞"		3⅞"	6	8	¾
B	48	3⅞" x 3⅞"		3⅞"	6	8	¾
C	48	2" x 3½"		3½"	3	20	⅜
D	48	2" x 3½"		3½"	3	20	⅜
Sashing Strips	31	1½" x 9½"		1½"	8	4	½
Set Squares	20	1½" x 1½"		1½"	1	24	⅛
Inner Border	2, 2	31½"	42"	¾"	4	—	⅛
Middle Border	2, 2	32"	45"	2"	4	—	⅓
Outer Border	2, 2	35"	51"	3½"	5	—	⅝
Lining	1	45" x 55"		—	—	—	1⅝*
Binding	1	2½" x 194"		2½"	6	—	½

*If fabric width after laundering is less than 44", lining will need to be pieced. Double yardage.

1. Place **A** and **B** right sides together, raw edges even. Mark a diagonal line from corner to corner and stitch ¼" on both sides of the marked line. Cut on the line to yield two **A-B** triangles units. Press seam allowances towards **B**.

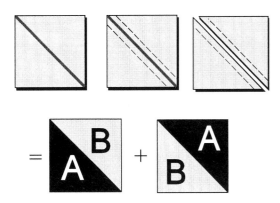

2. Join **C** and **D** patches. Stitch **C-D** units to photo-transfer and **A-B** triangle units to **C-D** units. Press seam allowances towards **C-D** units.

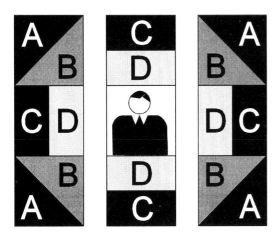

3. Join the three strips together to complete the block. Press seam allowances towards side strips.

4. Join blocks, sashing strips and set squares. Add borders.

Quilting Suggestion:

Black quilting thread in a traditional pattern will complete the "Amish" feel to this quilt. Echo quilt ¼" around each patch and stitch diagonal lines 1" apart in the border. Quilt two squares, one inside the other, centered on the set squares, to finish.

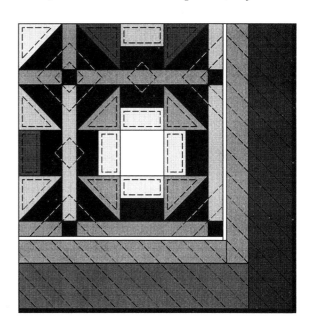

Log Cabin

#1

#2

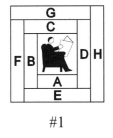

#1

#2

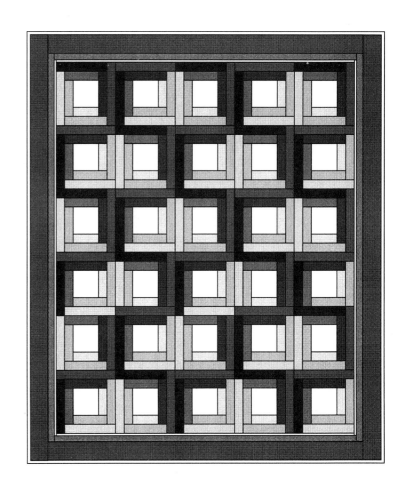

A single block, straight forward as block #1, turned sideways as block #2, combine to create this distinctive Log Cabin quilt. Strategically placed black buttons add a touch of whimsy. (See page 37.)
Quilt size: 43" x 50" • Finished block: 7" • Finished photo-transfer: 3" • Transfer paper: 5 sheets

CUTTING CHART

Patch/Sashing/Border	Quantity	Dimension		Strip Width	No. of Strips	Yield / Strip	Yards
Photo-transfer	30	3½" x 3½"		—	—	—	1
A	30	1½" x 3½"		1½"	4	8	¼
B, C	30, 30	1½" x 4½"		1½"	4, 4	8, 8	¼, ¼
D, E	30, 30	1½" x 5½"		1½"	8, 8	4, 4	½, ½
F, G	30, 30	1½" x 6½"		1½"	8, 8	4, 4	½, ½
H	30	1½" x 7½"		1½"	8	4	½
Inner Border	2, 2	35½"	43"	¾"	4	—	⅛
Middle Border	2, 2	36"	44½"	1¼"	4	—	¼
Outer Border	2, 2	37½"	49½"	3"	5	—	½
Lining	2	27½" x 47"		—	—	—	2¾
Binding	1	2½" x 196"		2½"	6	—	½

1. To make block #1, sew **A** to the *bottom* of each photo-transfer. To make block #2, sew **A** to the *right hand side* of the photo-transfer. Press seam allowances towards **A**. Add **B**. Press towards **B**.

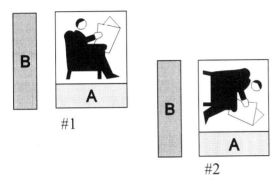

2. Add **C**, **D**, **E** and **F** working clockwise around the block. (Once **A** is sewn, the piecing strategy for both blocks is identical.) Press towards the new patches.

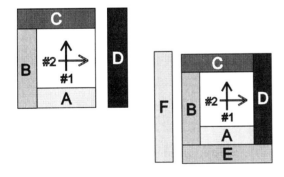

3. Add **G** and **H** to complete the block.

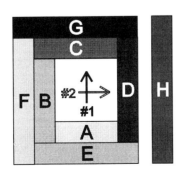

4. Make 15 block #1s and 15 block #2s. Join them in this array. Add borders and embellish with buttons.

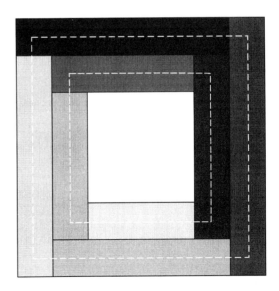

Quilting Suggestion:
*Quilt two squares, one inside the other. Stitch through the middle of **A-B-C-D** and then stitch through the middle of **E-F-G-H**.*

Shoo Fly

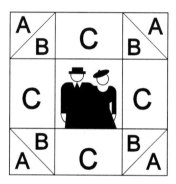

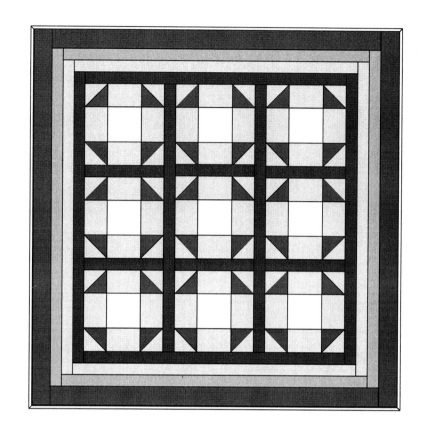

This delightful little wall quilt is as stunning as it is simple. Blocks are sashed with dark fabric and surrounded by four borders for a dramatic effect. The hardest part is deciding which nine photographs to use. (See page 38.)

Quilt size: 33" x 33" • Finished block: 7" • Finished photo-transfer: 3" • Transfer paper: 2 sheets

CUTTING CHART

Patch/Sashing/Border	Quantity	Dimension		Strip Width	No. of Strips	Yield / Strip	Yards
Photo-transfer	9	3½" x 3½"		—	—	—	1
A	36	2⅞" x 2⅞"		2⅞"	3	12	⅓
B	36	2⅞" x 2⅞"		2⅞"	3	12	⅓
C	36	2½" x 3½"		2½"	5	8	½
Sashing Strips	6, 2	7½"	23½"	1½"	3	—	¼
Dark Inner Border	2, 2	23½"	25½"	1½"	4	—	¼
Light Inner Border	2, 2	25½"	27½"	1½"	4	—	¼
Middle Border	2, 2	27½"	29½"	1½"	4	—	¼
Outer Border	2, 2	29½"	33"	2¼"	4	—	⅓
Lining	1	36" x 36"		—	—	—	1
Binding	1	2½" x 142"		2½"	4		⅓

1. Place **A** and **B** right sides together, raw edges even. Mark a diagonal line from corner to corner and stitch ¼" on both sides of the marked line. Cut on the line to yield two **A-B** triangles units. Press seam allowances towards **B**.

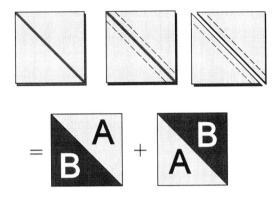

2. Stitch **C** to photo-transfer and sew **A-B** triangle units to **C** as shown. Press seam allowances towards **C**.

3. Join the three strips together to complete the block. Press seam allowances away from center strip.

4. Join blocks and sashing strips. Add borders.

Quilting Suggestion:

Try a curving quilting motif, like the one below, to contrast with the sharp, pointy lines of the patchwork. Plan it out with marking pencils, or stitch it totally free-form. Drop your feed dogs and have fun!

Log Window

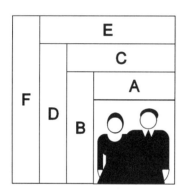

This combination of two traditional favorites looks like an Attic Window, but goes together like a Log Cabin. There are no set-in seams or mitred corners. Add "logs" from dark to light to create a wonderful three-dimensional effect. (See page 40.)

Quilt size: 47" x 54" • Finished block: 6" • Finished photo-transfer: 3" • Transfer paper: 5 sheets

CUTTING CHART

Patch/Sashing/Border	Quantity	Dimension		Strip Width	No. of Strips	Yield / Strip	Yards
Photo-transfer	30	3½" x 3½"		—	—	—	1
A	30	1½" x 3½"		1½"	4	8	¼
B	30	1½" x 4½"		1½"	4	8	¼
C	30	1½" x 4½"		1½"	4	8	¼
D	30	1½" x 5½"		1½"	8	4	½
E	30	1½" x 5½"		1½"	8	4	½
F	30	1½" x 6½"		1½"	8	4	½
Sashing Strips	24, 5	6½"	34½"	1½"	11	—	⅝
Light Inner Border	2, 2	34½"	43½"	1½"	4	—	¼
Dark Middle Border	2, 2	36½"	45½"	1½"	5	—	¼
Medium Outer Border	2, 2	38½"	53½"	4½"	6	—	⅞
Lining	2	29½" x 51"		—	—	—	2⅞
Binding	1	2½" x 212"		2½"	6	—	½

1. Sew **A** to the photo-transfer patch, pressing seam allowances towards **A**. Add patch **B** to the new unit. Press seam allowances towards **B**.

2. Sew patches **C** and **D** in the same manner. Press seam allowances towards the new "logs."

3. Add patches **E** and **F** to complete the block, pressing as before.

4. Join blocks and sashing strips. Add borders.

Quilting Suggestion:

In addition to any other quilting you may wish to do, quilt diagonally from the corner of the block to the photo-transfer to emphasize the illusion of depth.

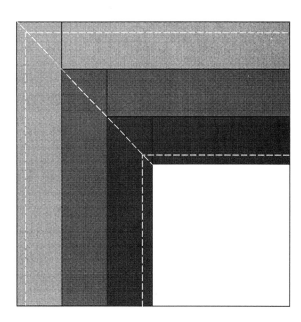

Spinning Windmill

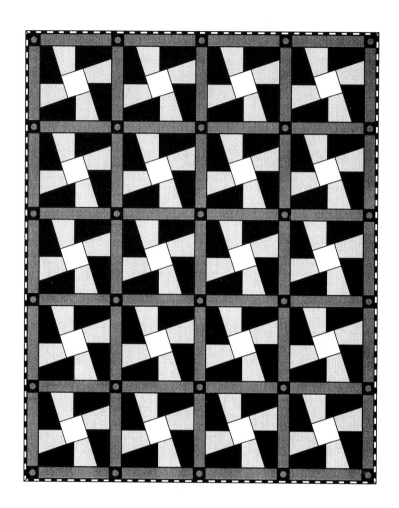

    Here's a twist! Yes, the center of the block is tilted at a slight angle to focus even more attention on the photo-transfer. Sashing strips and set squares surround each block and act as a border too. Self-covered buttons, appliqued circles, or in this case set squares "fussy-cut" from large polka dot fabric, become a secondary focal point. (See page 32.)
    Quilt size: 49" x 60" • Finished block: 9½" • Finished photo-transfer: 3" • Transfer paper: 4 sheets

CUTTING CHART

Patch/Sashing/Border	Quantity	Dimension	Strip Width	No. of Strips	Yield / Strip	Yards
Photo-transfer	20	3½" x 3½"	—	—	—	1
A	80	(see directions)	5¼"	9	(9)	1½
B	80	(see directions)	4"	9	(9)	1½
Sashing Strips	49	2½" x 10"	2½"	13	4	1
Set Squares	30	2½" x 2½"	2½"	2	16	¼
Lining	2	32½" x 53"	—	—	—	3
Binding	1	2½" x 228"	2½"	7	—	⅝

1. Sew strips **A** and **B** together as shown. Press towards darker fabric. From each **A-B** strip, cut 9 **A-B** units 4½" wide.

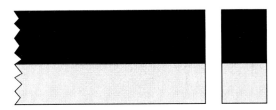

2. Remove the cutting template on page 79. Trim it, and tape it to the underside of a 6" x 12" ruler as shown.

   (Hint: use a ruler and a rotary cutter to trim away the excess paper from the template.)

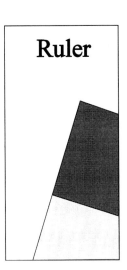

3. Position the cutting template on the **A-B** unit and trim the bottom and right side.

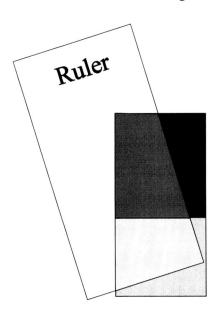

4. Partially stitch first **A-B** unit to photo-transfer as shown. Working counter-clockwise around photo-transfer, sew the next **A-B** unit. Press seam allowances away from photo-transfer.

5. Continue by adding the third **A-B** unit.

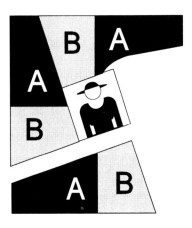

6. Add the last **A-B** unit and finish stitching the first seam to complete the block.

7. Join blocks, sashing strips and set
    squares.

Quilting Suggestion:

This block can be quilted with one continuous line of stitching. Follow the diagram below to quilt ¼" from each seam.

The sashing strips can be handled the same way, by quilting around each block. Those sashing strips nearest the borders will have to be quilted one side at a time.

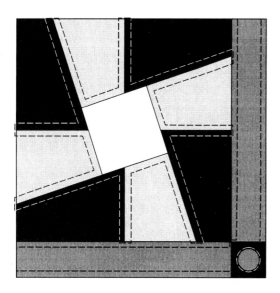

Resources

Transfer Paper & Supplies

Transfer Paper

Photos-To-Fabric® is a heat transfer paper developed for use in color copy machines. It can be ironed with a regular home iron. The resulting transfers are permanent, washable, and "iron-able." Originals are not harmed. Each sheet measures 8½" x 11" and is sold in packs of 6 or 12 pages. If it is not available at your local quilt or craft store, order directly from:

Mallery Press
4206 Sheraton Drive
Flint, MI 48532-3557
Toll free: (800)-278-4824
Outside US/Canada: (810) 733-8743
Fax: (810) 230-1516
E-mail: amisimms@aol.com
http://quilt.com/amisimms

Fabric

The best fabric to transfer onto is white 200 thread count cotton Springmaid Southern Belle or Kona 200 cotton. Both are widely available in quilt stores.*

Photo-Transferring Services

The companies listed below will transfer photographs to fabric for you.

Great American Quilt Factory
8970 East Hampden Ave.
Denver, CO 80231
Phone: (800) 474-2665
www.greatamericanquilt.com

photoTextiles
PO Box 3063
Bloomington, IN 47402
Toll free: (800) 388-3961

Additional Supplies, Patterns & Kits

Batting

The majority of quilts featured in this book were made with either Mountain Mist® Cotton Choice or HTC Fusible Fleece. Find these products in quilt or craft stores, or contact:

Stearns Technical Textile Company
100 Williams Street
Cincinnati, OH 45215
Toll free: (800) 345-7150
E-mail: stearns@fuse.net
www/palaver.com/mountainmist/

HTC Fusible Fleece
Handler Textile Corp.
60 Metro Way
Secaucus, NJ 07094
Phone: (201) 272-2000
Fax: (201) 272-2040
www.htc-handler.com

Big Foot®

This spring-loaded quilting foot lets you see where you're going.

Little Foot Ltd.
605 Bledsoe NW
Albuquerque, NM 87107
Phone: (505) 345-7647
Fax: (505) 345-4348
www.littlefoot.net

Lace Doilies

Look for lace doilies from Wimpole Street Creations at your craft store, or contact:

Barrett House
PO Box 540585
North Salt Lake, UT 84054-0585
Phone: (801) 299-0700

Mouse Pads & Coasters

White cloth, rubber-backed coasters and mouse pads can be found in large office supply and computer specialty stores.*

Paper-Backed Fusible Web

Pellon® Wonder-Under® is one of the few fusibles that are stitchable. It comes in regular and heavy weight. For more information about this product and where to purchase it in your area contact:

Fruedenberg Nonwovens
3440 Industrial Drive
Durham, NC 27704
Toll free: (800) 223-5275

Photo Quilt Blocks™

Currently available in five designs, kits include a laser cut foam block, transfer paper, white fabric to transfer on, sizing template, and complete instructions. Look for them in quilt shops*, or contact:

Quilt Majik™
13036 W. Anderson
Hayward, WI 54843
Toll free: (800) 476-6681

Teddy Bears

The teddy bears featured in this book were made with DreamSpinners pattern *#118...and the Three Bears* by Great American Quilt Factory, Inc. Patterns and instructions for 17", 20" and 24" bears are given. Find it at your quilt shop, or contact:

Great American Quilt Factory
8970 East Hampden Ave.
Denver, CO 80231
Phone: (800) 474-2665

(Mallery Press sells a kit featuring this pattern, Photos-To-Fabric® transfer paper, 200 thread count fabric to transfer on, and complete instructions.*)

Vests

Easy Reversible Vests by Carol Doak can be ordered directly from the publisher if it is not available at your local quilt shop:

That Patchwork Place
Martingale & Company
PO Box 118
Bothell, WA 98041-0118
Toll free: (800) 426-3126

Other Books By Ami Simms

Creating Scrapbook Quilts
Every Trick In The Book
How Not To Make A Prize-Winning Quilt
How To Improve Your Quilting Stitch
Invisible Applique

*The books listed above, as well as all items listed in the resource section marked with an asterisk (*), can be purchased directly from Mallery Press at the address below:

Mallery Press
4206 Sheraton Drive
Flint, MI 48532-3557
Toll free: 1-800-278-4824
Outside US/Canada: (810) 733-8743
Fax: (810) 230-1516
E-mail: amisimms@aol.com
http://quilt.com/amisimms

cut here

Cutting Template

For Spinning Windmill, page 74.
(Includes seam allowances.)

Notes